Korean Americans
A Concise History

Edward T. Chang and Carol K. Park

ISBN: 978-0-9982957-3-2 (sc)
ISBN: 978-0-9982957-4-9 (hc)
ISBN: 978-0-9982957-5-6 (e)

Library of Congress Control Number: 2019904540

The Young Oak Kim Center for Korean American Studies
at the University of California Riverside

900 University Avenue, #4031 CHASS INTN, Riverside, CA 92521

951-827-5661

Published with generous support from the Academy of Korean Studies
AKS-2014-INC-2230003.

Rev. Date: 05/30/2019

ACKNOWLEDGEMENTS

The teamwork and dedication that went into the production of this book were amazing. Over the last several years we've collected materials and original interviews of various Korean Americans whose stories informed our research and helped us contextualize this historical narrative.

We would like to thank the YOK Center donors and the pioneers of the Korean American community, including Ralph Ahn, for their support. We would also like to recognize and thank the Korean Americans who contributed to the independence of Korea during the early 1900s through their fundraising, public relations campaigns, and other activities. In particular, we want to acknowledge and highlight the Korean American women who contributed to the independence movement through their leadership, hard work, support, and organization.

We would also like to extend our sincerest gratitude to Dr. Myung Ki "Mike" Hong for his patronage and his continued belief in the YOK Center and our endeavors. Also, we would like to thank the Catherine Violet Kim estate and its executor Meiko Inaba for the generous contribution of photographs, primary source materials, and other documents that aided in our research. We also want to thank Kyung Won "K.W." Lee for his inspirational contributions to our community through his journalism and guidance.

We also thank the YOK Center, UC Riverside interns who helped to collect and gain permission for the use of the images presented in this book: Ulises Perez, Jacqueline Aguirre De La O, Crystal Mariano, and Hyeri Victoria Jeon. Finally, we thank the Academy of Korean Studies for its generous support of this publication.

INTRODUCTION

Understanding the history of Korea is an important stepping stone necessary to properly tell the Korean American story. While much of Korean American history is tied to Korea, it is essential to note that Korean American history is also a unique, separate narrative.

Korean American history can be traced back to 1882, when the United States of America and the Kingdom of Korea, signed a treaty known as the Treaty of Peace, Amity, Commerce, and Navigation. A very small number of Korean ginseng merchants landed in San Francisco, California, in the late 1800s. However, official Korean immigration to the U.S. began on January 13, 1903, when a group of Koreans boarded the *S.S. Gaelic* and sailed to Honolulu, Hawaii. One hundred and two of those pioneering Koreans labored on Hawaiian sugar plantations. By 1905, the number of Koreans in Hawaii swelled to 7,226.[1] Today, the United States celebrates January 13 as Korean American Day.

The early Korean American community focused its time and efforts on the independence of their homeland. At the end of the Russo-Japanese War in 1905, Korea became a protectorate of Japan. By 1910, Japan had colonized and obtained Korea and the peninsula became part of the Japanese Empire. It would remain under Japanese rule until 1945. Koreans living in the United States considered themselves nationals and organized meetings and rallies for the freedom of their homeland. They also gathered funds and published newspapers. Korean Americans also lobbied the United States government for political support and recognition of Korea as a separate nation during the 1930s and early 1940s with little success.

---

[1] Choy, Bong-youn. *Koreans in America*. Chicago: Nelson Hall Press, 1979. 92-94.

She gets 50¢ a day for cutting sugar

A worker cuts sugar cane in Hawaii, earning about 50 cents a day.
Image circa 1920 and courtesy of the Korean American Digital Archive,
Digital Library, University of Southern California. (USC)

Koreans living in Hawaii and on the U.S. mainland established churches and various associations to aide in the independence movement. Syngman Rhee and Dosan Ahn Chang Ho were two of the main leaders in the Korean American community at the time. Their work, especially Dosan Ahn Chang Ho's, shaped the identities and structure of the early Korean community in America.

During World War I (1914-1918), several Koreans joined the fight as American soldiers, hoping to learn combat skills they could later utilize in a fight against Japan. During the early 1900s, Korean American identity was strongly tied to their nationalism. In 1920, a group of Koreans established a combat pilot training school in Willows, California. The school trained Korean pilots who believed their aviation skills could aide in the independence of their homeland. The Willows Korean Aviation School and Corps graduated Korea's first two aviation officers in 1921.

When World War II broke out in 1939, several hundred Korean Americans, including Colonel (Col.) Young Oak Kim, answered the call of duty and fought on the front lines for the United States. Col. Kim became a war hero and a highly decorated U.S. Army officer for his actions, bravery, and leadership. Many Korean Americans fought in the war because they believed they were helping Korea as well.

After the end of World War II in 1945, Korea regained its place on the world map as an independent nation. However, the country was divided into South Korea and North Korea at the 38th parallel in 1945. In 1948, Syngman Rhee became the leader of the Republic of Korea in the south, and Kim Il-Sung became the dictator of the communist Democratic People's Republic of Korea (DPRK) in the north.

Two years later, on June 25, 1950, the North invaded the South and started the Korean War, which lasted from 1950 to 1953. The United States backed South Korea, and the Soviet Union and China supported North Korea. Bloody and horrific battles were fought on the Korean Peninsula. Korean nationals living in America joined the fight as U.S. soldiers. Col. Kim, who had reenlisted so he could fight for his mother country, became the first minority (non-white) battalion commander during active combat in the history of the U.S. Army.

Many Koreans, Korean Americans, and Americans died during the war. The Korean War technically never ended but only came to a standstill after an armistice agreement was signed on July 27, 1953. By the end of the Korean War, about 2.9 million American troops, North and South Korean civilians and military, and Chinese armed forces, had perished.[2] The war also separated more than 10 million families.

Today, the Korean American population is dispersed throughout the United States. The U.S. Census Bureau estimated the total Korean

---

[2] Millet, Allan R. "Korean War." *Encyclopedia Britannica*. June 18, 2018. www.britannica.com/event/Korean-War.

American population at nearly 1.9 million in 2017.[3] The highest concentration of Korean Americans resides in Los Angeles County, California, where the population reached 215,238 in 2017.[4] Symbolically, the heart of the Korean American community is in Los Angeles. Known as Koreatown, this transnational enclave gained popularity over the years. By the early 2000s, Korean culture and food hit mainstream American society hard. Korean barbecue, Korean dramas and music, and even Korean American actors, like John Cho, Sandra Oh, Steven Yeun, and Randall Park, took the American pop culture scene by surprise.

However, it is important to note that, while Korean Americans are visible in American society, this was not always the case. The Korean American story is a multifaceted tale of hardship and triumph. From the occupation of Korea by Japan to the Korean War in 1950, Korean Americans have suffered and endured a myriad of trials and tribulations.

Korean immigration to the United States began to increase dramatically after the passage of the 1965 Immigration Act. The act essentially allowed for more Koreans and other Asians to immigrate to America under fewer restrictions. During the 1970s, a high number of Koreans moved to the United States. Many of these new urban immigrants were brought over by Korean war brides; the wives of American soldiers who fought in the Korean War. The so called "G.I. Brides" sponsored their family members to come to the United States under the new provisions of the 1965 Immigration Act. By 1980, the Korean American population had reached 354,953. By 1990, that number would more than double to 798,849.[5] In

---

[3] "Table B02018: Asian Alone or in Any Combination by Selected Groups. Universe: Total Asian Alone or in Any Combination Population. 2017 American Community Survey 1-Year Estimates." U.S. Census Bureau. Accessed January 4, 2019. https://factfinder.census.gov/faces/tableservices/jsf/pages/productview.xhtml?pid=ACS_17_1YR_B02018&prodType=table.

[4] "Table DP05: ACS Demographic and Housing Estimates. 2013-2017 American Community Survey 5-Year Estimates." U.S. Census Bureau. Accessed February 28, 2019. https://factfinder.census.gov/faces/tableservices/jsf/pages/productview.xhtml?src=CF.

[5] Min, Pyong Gap, and Chigon Kim. "Growth of the Korean Population and Changes in Their Settlement Patterns Over Time, 1990-2008." Research Center for Korean Community, Queens College of CUNY, Research Report No. 2 (March 16, 2010).

2000, Korean Americans totaled 1.2 million, and by 2010, that number reached 1.7 million. (See Table 1).[6]

Table 1[7]

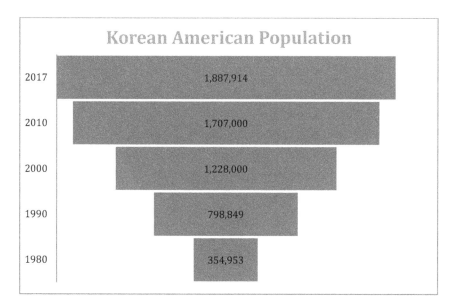

Despite their growing numbers, Korean immigrants found it difficult to adjust to life in America, as they faced language barriers and cultural differences. Due to discrimination and racism, Koreans had limited options for employment. Many were pigeonholed into running small businesses such as liquor stores, wig shops, grocery stores, and even gas stations. Many of them opened shops in inner-city communities in states including California, New York, and Illinois. Korean immigrants were denied corporate jobs and found themselves stuck in the position of the middleman minority in the United States. The *middleman minority theory* suggests that the group occupying the buffer between the so-called dominant and subordinate groups is hated and not trusted by the lower group. In this example, Korean Americans were the middlemen between the white community (seen as dominant) and African American and Latino

---

[6] "Koreans in the U.S. Fact Sheet." Pew Research Center. September 8, 2017. www.pewsocialtrends.org/fact-sheet/asian-americans-koreans-in-the-u-s/.
[7] Ibid.

communities (seen as subordinate). Thus, Korean Americans were praised by white Americans as the "model minority," though they were not offered corporate jobs, and despised by the African American community and seen as rude and disrespectful. Korean Americans were caught in the middle of a precarious situation.

During the 1980s the conflict between black Americans and Korean Americans was at the center of national media attention. Many Korean Americans found themselves blamed for the rising racial tension. Shootings, robberies, and other incidents of violence were directed toward Korean shop owners. After the shooting of Latasha Harlins by Korean store owner Soon Ja Du in March 1991, crimes against Korean merchants escalated. By late March 1992, ten Korean merchants had been killed during robberies.

Arson fires destroyed five Korean-owned shops in Los Angeles in a six-month period from late 1990 to early 1991.[8] Hate crimes against Korean Americans also increased. Nineteen Korean Americans were victims of hate crimes in 1991, as well as the number-one Asian group in Los Angeles to be victimized by hate crimes. (In 1991, 54 hate crimes were reported in Los Angeles and 19 were against Korean Americans.[9])

The voiceless Korean American community had little to no representation in U.S. politics. The small community, which barely made up one million people compared to an overall U.S. population of 253 million at the time, was often looked over. With marginal representation in government offices, Korean Americans were forced to rely on their churches, friends, and family to help them.

With this scene set, Korean Americans became the scapegoat of the 1992 L.A. Riots; this event occurred after four L.A. police officers were found not guilty for the crime of violently beating African American Rodney King. Blamed for taking jobs, charging too much for inferior products, and not understanding or assimilating well into American culture, Korean Americans found themselves in a position that would later work against them.

---

[8] Lee, John H. "Bullets End Immigrant's Struggle: Crime: A Korean shopkeeper found shot to death in her car had striven for two decades to make a new life. Now her husband is left to wonder what it was all for." *Los Angeles Times,* April 7, 1992. http://articles.latimes.com/1992-04-07/local/me-692_1_los-angeles-korean-media.

[9] Ibid.

Korean Americans were left to defend themselves when the Los Angeles Police Department abandoned Koreatown during the 1992 L.A. Riots, according to journalist K.W. Lee. On the news, many Korean Americans were shown on the rooftops of their businesses with guns, battling would-be looters. Non-Korean shop owners put up signs in their store windows that said, "Latino Owned" or "Black Owned." The media portrayed Koreans as gun-toting vigilantes instead of Korean immigrants fighting to protect their American Dreams from going up in flames. Koreans relied on ethnic media, like Radio Korea, for information. In fact, Radio Korea served as a lifeline for Korean immigrants during the Los Angeles Riots of 1992.

The real issues that surrounded the six days of violence were ignored by the mainstream U.S. news media. These issues included differences in social and financial status, police brutality, racism, discrimination, drugs, gangs, a lack of education, and government neglect, among various other problems. The Rodney King verdict was the match that lit the fuse to a keg of dynamite that had long been stuck in a back room, waiting to explode. When all was said and done, the riots took more than 50 lives including that of one Korean American: Edward Song Lee. Of the $1 billion in damages, Korean Americans suffered 40 percent of the losses. Many Korean Americans lost their livelihood and never recovered from it.

For the Korean American community, the psychological repercussions of the L.A. Riots far outweighed the physical destruction. Today, Korean Americans who lived through the L.A. Riots suffer from post-traumatic stress disorder (PTSD) and depression. However, not all was lost. The Korean community in America emerged from the chaos of the 1992 L.A. Riots with a new sense of identity. Like a phoenix reborn from the ashes, the Korean American community regained its voice.

After the riots, Koreans in the U.S. began to rethink their identity, learned many valuable lessons, and began to rebuild. The riots served as a catalyst for the community to critically re-examine what it meant to be Korean American in relation to multiracial politics and society. The early Korean American community viewed themselves as Korean nationals, a people without a home, but after the L.A. Riots, Koreans in America recognized that their identity was tied to their host country, the United States. They began to view themselves as Korean Americans, not Korean nationals.

After the riots, Korean Americans became more vocal and participated in politics, gave back to their communities, built coalitions, and strived to be more visible in their towns and cities. As a result, Korean Americans are no longer the unrecognized business owners of yesteryear. Now, Koreans are part of mainstream America. Despite the difficult history Korean Americans have suffered through, they are now business owners, citizens, teachers, lawyers, community activists, war heroes, and so much more. To understand Korean American history properly, we must look at the people and heroes who helped shape this small ethnic community into what it is today.

CHAPTER 1

EARLY KOREAN AMERICANS & THE HAWAIIAN SUGAR PLANTATIONS

Official Korean immigration to the United States began on January 13, 1903, when the *S.S. Gaelic* transported 102 Koreans to Hawaii, a territory of the United States at the time.[10] The pioneering Koreans lived and worked on sugar and pineapple farms. How and why did Koreans go to Hawaii to work on these plantations? Before delving further into these questions, it's important to understand the events that led up to 1903.

In 1883, after the signing of the Treaty of Amity, Commerce and Navigation, also known as the Shufeldt Treaty—a treaty between Korea and the United States that allowed Koreans to pursue opportunities in the United States and for Americans to enter Korea—the first official envoy from Korea visited America.

The Korean envoy was led by Min Young-ik,[11] who stayed in the United States instead of returning to Korea. Min was the first Korean student to study in America. He attended the Governor Drummer Academy in Massachusetts.[12] Two years after the first envoy from Korea sojourned to

---

[10] Page 1. *The San Francisco Call*, January 14, 1903.

[11] Note, the spelling and identification of the Korean names presented in the textbook typically follow one of two types: 1) Last Name, First name as in Ahn Chang Ho or like Park Yoeng-hyo; 2) First Name, Last Name as in Syngman Rhee. The name spellings are based on how they were presented in historic records.

[12] *Korean Experience Chronology in the United States.* Gwacheon, South Korea: National Institute for Korean History, 2010, 10-12.

America, another group of Koreans decided to visit. In 1885, Soh Jae Pil, Park Yoeng-hyo, and Seo Gwang-beom boarded a ship and sailed to San Francisco. Although Soh Jae Pil lived and worked in the United States, he was not officially counted by the US government as a Korean immigrant. The first recorded Korean immigrant to the United States is believed to be Peter Ryu; he arrived in Honolulu in 1901.[13]

A typical sugar cane field with laborers in Hawaii in 1920. Image courtesy of the Korean American Digital Archive, Digital Library, USC.

The signing of the Shufeldt Treaty and the opening of the doors of Korea allowed a U.S. diplomatic delegation to enter the land once known as the "Hermit Kingdom." In 1884, Dr. Horace Allen, a Protestant minister and medical doctor, was one of the first Americans to officially enter the Korean peninsula.[14] Dr. Allen learned Korean culture and became a close and trusted advisor to the last ruling monarch of the country; King Kojong of Korea. Nearly 20 years later, Dr. Allen would play an instrumental role in starting Korean emigration to the United States. However, Koreans were not the first Asians to migrate to America. The Chinese

---

[13] Ibid, 24.
[14] Patterson, Wayne. *The Korean Frontier in America: Immigration to Hawaii, 1896–1910*. Honolulu: University of Hawaii Press, 1988. 19-20.

American community was well established by the late 1800s. The Gold Rush of 1849 and the construction of the Transcontinental Railroad in the U.S. attracted Chinese immigrants.[15] Thus, Chinese American communities were established in various areas of the United States, including San Francisco, California. The Chinese American communities offered intrepid Koreans an opportunity. In the late 1800s, a handful of Korean ginseng merchants made their way to Hawaii and San Francisco hoping to sell to the Chinese living there.

In 1902, the Hawaiian Sugar Plantation Association (HSPA) decided to recruit a new labor force. The HSPA already had Chinese, Portuguese, and Japanese workers. However, the HSPA feared the workers would unionize and demand higher wages and better working conditions. Many of the Japanese workers also "deserted" their plantation lives and moved to the mainland.[16] Thus, the HSPA decided to diversify the workforce. At first, they used laborers from Puerto Rico. In 1901, the HSPA hired about 6,000 Puerto Ricans.[17] But the new laborers proved to be unreliable as well. Thus, the HSPA turned to Koreans. The HSPA sent David Deshler as its representative to Korea. With the help of Dr. Allen, Deshler set up a bank in Korea to help fund emigrants' passage to the U.S., gained permission from Korean officials to recruit workers, and sent the first 121 Koreans to Hawaii; they arrived on January 13, 1903. After medical examination, only 102 of those 121 passengers aboard the *S.S. Gaelic*, were permitted to stay, thus marking the official start of Korean immigration to the United States.

Deshler, who illegally bypassed U.S. labor laws, helped ship thousands of pioneering Koreans to the Hawaiian Islands. By 1905, Hawaii was home to 7,226 Koreans. In that same year, Korea became a protectorate of Japan, and the Japanese government, in order to protect the economic interests of its laborers, prohibited further Korean emigration to Hawaii. Instead, some of the Koreans who had first arrived from 1903 to 1905, returned to their homeland either to stay or to bring their wives and children back

---

[15] Higham, John. *Strangers in the Land: Patterns of American Nativism, 1860–1925*, 2nd ed. New Brunswick, N.J.: Rutgers University Press, 1988. 25.

[16] Patterson, Wayne. *The Korean Frontier in America: Immigration to Hawaii, 1896–1910*. Honolulu: University of Hawaii Press, 1988. 12-13.

[17] Ibid.

to America. Some even brought back new brides and started families in Hawaii.[18]

The story of Korean immigration to the United States has been documented by Wayne Patterson, who in 1988 penned *The Korean Frontier in America: Immigration to Hawaii, 1896–1910.* According to Patterson, the Koreans that came to Hawaii differed from the Chinese and Japanese immigrants. While most of the Chinese and Japanese immigrants were farmers from rural areas, the Korean immigrants came from cities, and more than half of them were from the Seoul-Incheon-Suwon area.[19] The Koreans who came to the United States to work on the Hawaiian plantations included a variety of low- to high-class men; some were highly educated, and some were not. The men were between the ages of twenty and thirty and single, according to Patterson. However, many of the Korean immigrants shared one common aspect: the Christian faith.

The Koreans that migrated to Hawaii did so for four main reasons according to Patterson: (1) attaining a fortune and a better life, (2) an education, (3) political freedom, and (4) religious freedom, the last of which explains the role Christianity played in Korean emigration to the U.S. Many had heard stories of America and the western way of life. Presbyterian missionaries helped to promote this view of America, and many Koreans converted to Christianity.[20] Missionaries influenced their Korean converts and taught them that America was the promised land where they could find better lives and opportunity. Thus, quite a few of those pioneering Koreans who went to Hawaii were Christians, and many of those who were not converted to the faith after arriving at the sugar plantations.

Once Koreans arrived in Hawaii, they were faced with hardship. Wages were low at about 70 cents per day.[21] Under the supervision of a "luna," or foreman, Koreans toiled in the fields from dawn to dusk and

---

[18] Chang, Roberta, and Wayne Patterson. *The Koreans in Hawai'i: A Pictorial History 1903–2003.* Honolulu: University of Hawai'i Press, 2003. 74.

[19] Patterson, Wayne. *The Korean Frontier in America: Immigration to Hawaii, 1896–1910.* Honolulu: University of Hawaii Press, 1988. 103.

[20] Ibid, 105-109.

[21] Patterson, Wayne. *The Korean Frontier in America: Immigration to Hawaii, 1896–1910.* Honolulu: University of Hawaii Press, 1988. 106.

lived on plantation-owned barracks or cottages. Despite the hard labor, Koreans made time to worship, and in April 1905, the Korean Methodist Church was officially founded and recognized by the superintendent of the Hawaii Methodist Church. The Korean Methodist Church served as a gathering place for Koreans to worship, socialize, and discuss the independence of their home country. However, because the church was not a formal settlement and because laborers lived in barracks owned by the plantations they worked on, Koreans in Hawaii were not yet organized into an official, autonomous community.

Korean laborers in Hawaii left after about a year or two of their arrival in 1903. The U.S. mainland enticed the Koreans with promises of higher wages from railroad and farm work, better living conditions, and other opportunities. Some Koreans were living in California by 1904, but from 1905 to 1907, approximately 1,300 Koreans made their way to San Francisco. The bustling port city offered Koreans information on jobs and served as a stepping stone. According to scholar and Professor Youn-Cha Chey:

> Between 1905 and 1907, before the passage of the Oriental Exclusion Act of 1924, about 1,[3]00 Korean plantation workers entered San Francisco. San Francisco was a temporary station for Koreans from Hawaii, where they could obtain job information to settle in the mainland. From San Francisco, they dispersed along the west coast to Sacramento and Riverside and became farm workers in California.[22]

Koreans who stayed in San Francisco established the Korean Methodist Church of San Francisco in October 1905. While it served as a gathering place for the scattered Korean population living in San Francisco, it did not constitute an organized settlement either. Instead, Koreans lived with the Chinese in the already established Chinatown in San Francisco. The high anti-Asian sentiment in San Francisco made the area less hospitable for the newly arriving Koreans. Though some of the Koreans who went to San

---

[22] Chey, Youn-Cha S. "100-Year History of Korean Immigration to America." *A Historical Profile of San Francisco's Korean Community Development*. September 25, 2002. www.iic.edu/Main/AboutUs/ImmigrationHistoryYChey.htm#ft5

Francisco from Hawaii moved on to Southern California and other states like Wyoming, New Jersey, and even Mississippi, much of the Korean American population lived and worked in California.

In the first half of the twentieth century, Koreans in the United States worked fervently for the independence of their homeland. In fact, from 1905 to 1945, early Korean American identity was defined by Korean nationalism; that is, Koreans in America viewed themselves as a people without a country. In 1905, Japan declared Korea as a protectorate of its empire. By 1910, Japan formally colonized Korea and Koreans lost their sovereignty. Prior to the colonization and occupation of Korea, the Japanese Meiji government was already involved and interfering with the Korean government and its people. Japan dominated Korea through politics, strict control, and through economic exploitation. The Treaty of Ganghwa Island in 1876 opened trade, declared that Korea was no longer a tributary state to China, and allowed Japanese citizens to travel to Korea and conduct business. The treaty also called for open surveying of the Korean coast by Japanese ships. This would be the beginning of Japan's influence over Korea and eventually, the fall of the Korean government.

Korean leaders, including Ahn Chang Ho and Syngman Rhee, made their way to the United States prior to the occupation and colonization of their homeland. On October 14, 1902, Ahn arrived in the United States with his wife Helen (Hye-ryon). After taking the wrong ship and traveling through Vancouver, Canada,[23] and Seattle,[24] Ahn and his wife finally arrived in San Francisco. Penniless, they wandered around San Francisco's Chinatown where they met Dr. Alessandro D. Drew, who had once served as a missionary in Korea. Dr. Drew took Ahn and his wife in and helped them get back on their feet. Ahn, whose penname is Dosan, or Island Mountain, came to the United States hoping to learn English, western ideals, and democratic principles. Later, Dosan would use his western education to help the Korean independence movement which shaped and guided the early Korean American community's activities, identity, and way of life.

---

[23] "Corea the Sleeping Land: Its Queer People. Strange Customs and Coming Awakening." *San Francisco Chronicle,* December 7, 1902. Page 11.

[24] Dosan Ahn Chang Ho's passport shows a Seattle stamp prior to his arrival to San Francisco in 1902.

Korean Picture Brides: Women of Strength

Starting in 1910, Korean women emigrated to the United States as picture brides. Though they usually had not met in person, these women married Korean men in Hawaii after an exchange of letters, photographs, and family approvals. Korean picture brides brought a sense of stability and structure to the lives of the bachelor men who worked on the Hawaiian plantations. The Gentlemen's Agreement of 1907 between the U.S. and Japan lifted the ban on Korean immigration and allowed Korean immigrants to bring immediate family members to America. Korean laborers in Hawaii therefore brought their spouses, children, siblings, and parents. Many of the Korean bachelors also brought picture brides.

During the early 1900s, Korean picture brides often sent
photos to bachelors similar to the one above.

From 1909 to 1924 about 950 Korean women, including picture brides, made their way to Hawaii.[25] Picture-bride marriages were arranged through various means. Sometimes a matchmaker was consulted, and pictures and letters were exchanged. Other picture-bride marriages resulted from family agreements and arrangements. Some Korean bachelors utilized the help of friends to find their wives. The picture brides found themselves not only marrying men they hardly knew, but once they arrived, they were faced with harsh working and living conditions. Many of these women not only cleaned, cooked, and took care of the children, they also earned money doing side jobs. They supported their husbands in their independence movement activities and struggled to better their circumstances.

The story of one of these picture brides, Lee Young Oak, was well documented by Won K. Yoon in his book, *The Passage of a Picture Bride*. Born on October 25, 1901, Lee was 15 years old when she was approached by a matchmaker in Korea. She was enthralled by the idea of going to America, finding a husband, and making a good living. When it was proposed that she marry a Korean bachelor in Hawaii, Lee readily agreed. Photos and letters were exchanged. Excited by the prospect of a new life and a strange new land, Lee boarded a ship to Honolulu, Hawaii. When she arrived, she met her husband-to-be, Mr. Chung Bong Woon.

Mr. Chung had worked in Hawaii for 15 years before he finally decided to get married. When his wife-to-be arrived, he was happy. Once they were married, they spent their honeymoon in Honolulu and were praised by the local Korean innkeepers. For years, the innkeepers witnessed countless picture-bride unions end in turmoil, sadness, and strife.[26] After the honeymoon, Lee followed her husband back to the Maui plantation where he worked. Together, they had six boys and remained in Hawaii where they supported the Korean independence movement. They even became instrumental followers of Syngman Rhee.

The height of the Korean picture bride years lasted from 1913 to 1919. The families these women raised would later become integral parts of

---

[25] Chang, Roberta, and Wayne Patterson. *The Koreans in Hawai'i: A Pictorial History 1903–2003*. Honolulu: University of Hawai'i Press, 2003. 79.

[26] Yook, Won K. *The Passage of a Picture Bride*. Loma Linda, California: Pacific Rim Press, 1994. 55.

Hawaii's Korean American community. However, picture bride exchanges stopped after the signing of the Johnson-Reed Act, or the Immigration Act of 1924. The law included the National Origins Act and the Asian Exclusion Act, which prohibited Asian immigration to the United States.

Korean American Highlight
Philip Jaisohn: The First Korean American Citizen

Philip Jaisohn at Washington D.C.'s Union Depot in 1922.
Image courtesy of the Korean American Digital Archive, Digital Library, USC.

Soh Jae Pil was born in Kanae Village, Boseong County, Korea, on January 7, 1864. He was the second son of a Korean magistrate. When he came to the United States, Soh wanted to maintain his Korean identity and decided to change his name to Philip Jaisohn, which is his Korean name spelled backwards. Jaisohn studied in Japan and advocated for modernizing Korea. In 1884, Jaisohn participated in the Kapsin Coup, a three-day coup d'état. Reformers moved to eliminate social distinctions based on the legal privileges of the higher *yangban* class. The *yangban* were Korea's elite, educated, ruling class. Led by the political faction known as the Progressives, the coup failed and Jaisohn fled Korea.[27] In 1885, he migrated to the United States.

The pioneering Jaisohn was the first Korean to obtain American citizenship in 1890. A studious individual, he attended Harry Hillman Academy in Wilkes-Barre, Pennsylvania. In 1892, Jaisohn graduated from Columbian College in Washington, D.C., which is known as George Washington University today. He earned a medical degree and became a practicing physician. About two years after he became a doctor, he met and married Muriel Armstrong, the niece of former U.S. President James Buchanan, with whom he had two children.[28]

Dr. Jaisohn worked fervently for his motherland, hoping to shape policies and later, to help free it from Japanese occupation. In 1895, the Korean government requested that Dr. Jaisohn return to his homeland as an advisor. While living and working in Korea, he established the Independence Club and advocated for education reforms. He strongly advocated the use of *hangul*, the Korean alphabet system invented by King Sejong the Great in 1446, primarily by starting a paper written in Korean for the Korean people. He succeeded in his effort when in 1896, Dr. Jaisohn began publishing *The Independence*, which was written in *hangul*. In Korea, he was known as a highly accomplished individual, involved in several projects including the construction of the Independence Hall and the Independence Gate in 1897.

However, Dr. Jaisohn's activities raised the ire of the Korean monarchy and its officials, who accused him of plotting to overthrow the Korean government. In 1898, though the Korean government asked Dr. Jaisohn to

---

[27] Chang, Roberta, and Wayne Patterson. *The Koreans in Hawai'i: A Pictorial History 1903–2003*. Honolulu: University of Hawai'i Press, 2003. 8.

[28] Liem, Channing. *The First Korean-American—A Forgotten Hero: Philip Jaisohn.* Philadelphia: Philip Jaisohn Memorial Foundation, 1984.

return to the United States, he continued working toward the betterment of the Korean government, and later, toward Korean independence. In April 1919, he convened the First Korean Congress in Philadelphia after he heard about the March First Mansei movement in Korea. The movement was an independence rally held by Koreans against Japanese rule of their homeland; Koreans all over the world were inspired to act and supported the movement with donations, protests, and more.

In his later years, Dr. Jaisohn raised his family and conducted medical research at the University of Pennsylvania. He opened a medical practice in 1936, wrote research articles, and even volunteered as a U.S. Army physical exam officer during World War II. He would not see his homeland again until 1947. He served as chief advisor to the U.S. Military Government after World War II and was also a member of the Korean Interim Legislative Assembly. Dr. Jaisohn pushed for reform and unification of North and South Korea at the time, but after serving for one year in Korea, Dr. Jaisohn returned to the United States where he lived until his death on January 5, 1951.[29]

---

[29] Ibid.

Korean American Highlight
Syngman Rhee

Syngman Rhee as a young man. Image courtesy of the Korean
American Digital Archive, Digital Library, USC.

Born on March 26, 1875, in Pyongsan, Hwanghae Province, in what
is now North Korea, Syngman Rhee was the first president of the Republic
of Korea (South Korea). As a boy, he studied in Seoul and learned English
while attending a Methodist school in Korea. Rhee was a Korean independence activist, for which he was arrested and imprisoned from 1898-1904.
Upon his release in November 1904, he made his way to the United States.
In 1910, Rhee graduated with a Ph.D. in history, politics, and economics
from Princeton University,[30] making him the first Korean to earn a doctorate degree from an American university. He returned to Korea for two
years, and after serving as a YMCA coordinator and missionary, he traveled
back to the United States in 1912. Rhee resided in Hawaii and traveled the
world, fighting for the independence of Korea.

Ideologically, he butted heads with Dosan Ahn Chang Ho and Koreans
were divided by their support of the two individuals. He would also later
disagree with his friend and Korean independence activist Park Yong-man,

---

[30] Looper, John De. "Syngman Rhee's Time at Princeton." March 1, 2011. https://
blogs.princeton.edu/mudd/2011/03/syngman-rhees-time-at-princeton/.

on foreign relations. During his first few years in Hawaii, Rhee established the Han-in Christian Church and published the *Pacific Magazine*.[31] In 1919, Rhee and Seo Jae Pil (Philip Jaisohn) held the First Korean Congress in Philadelphia.

In 1919, Rhee was elected prime minister of the Korean Provisional Government (KPG) in Shanghai.[32] In 1921, he established the Korean Comrade Association (Dongji Hoe). Rhee left Shanghai in 1922 and returned to the United States, where he focused on his independence efforts, religion, and education. By 1925, Rhee was impeached by members of the Korean Provisional Government in Shanghai over misuse of power. However, Rhee continued to misrepresent himself as the KPG's president and conducted his independence activities through the Hansung Provisional Government and the Korean Commission to America and Europe. Rhee established the Korean Christian Church and other schools and organizations during his time in Hawaii. In 1933, he represented the interests of Korea at the League of Nations conference in Geneva. In 1934, he married Franziska Donner whom he had met at the Geneva convention.

Rhee worked with the Office of Strategic Services in anti-Japanese activities, and in 1945, he represented Korea at the United Nations Conference on International Organization. After the end of World War II and the surrender of Japan on September 2, 1945, Rhee returned to Korea. For three years, Rhee worked to raise his position through various activities, and on July 20, 1948, he was elected president of the Republic of (South) Korea, which was formally established on August 15, 1948.

Rhee's presidency was riddled with controversy. Rhee's actions during the Korean War (1950–1953), drew criticism from the international community. The December Massacres of 1950, for instance, tarnished his name. The massacres were politically motivated executions ordered by the

---

[31] Fields, David P. "Syngman Rhee: Socialist." Cold War International History Project: Working Papers. No. 82. Woodrow Wilson International Center for Scholars, Washington D.C. June 2017.

[32] Wilson Center Digital Archive: International History Declassified. Biographies: Syngman Rhee, First President of South Korea from 1948-1960. https://digita-larchive.wilsoncenter.org/resource/modern-korean-history-portal/syngman-rhee/biography

Rhee regime after South Korean forces recaptured Pyongyang in North Korea. Thousands of suspected communists and prisoners were killed.[33]

When the armistice negotiations began, Rhee was opposed to the talks.[34] However, the armistice was agreed upon on July 27, 1953, by the U.S.-led United Nations Command, North Korea, and China. After the war, Rhee would continue his controversial presidency. He was re-elected in 1952 and again in 1956, which should have been his last term. However, Rhee had the constitution amended so that he could run for an unlimited amount of terms. In 1960, Rhee won his fourth presidency. Rhee's choice for vice president, Lee Ki-poong, was elected to office the same year. However, the opposing Democratic Party claimed the election was rigged by Rhee, and a demonstration was held in Masan, Korea. Authorities shot the demonstrators and thus sparked a student-led revolution on April 19, 1960. Demonstrators forced the resignation of Rhee on April 26, 1960. Rhee and his wife were flown out of Korea on April 28 to Hawaii, where they lived in exile in Honolulu. Rhee authored several books in his lifetime including *The Spirit of Independence* and *Japan Inside Out*. On July 19, 1965, Rhee died from a stroke. He was accepted back into his motherland to be buried at Seoul National Cemetery.

---

[33] "Mass Executions by Southerners: Bitter Resentment by U.K. Troops in Korea." *The West Australian*, December 18, 1950. Page 1.
[34] "Syngman Rhee: First President of South Korea." CNN.com. http://www.cnn.com/fyi/school.tools/profiles/Syngman.Rhee/content.html. Accessed March 7, 2019.

CHAPTER 2

PACHAPPA CAMP AND NOTEWORTHY KOREAN AMERICAN INCIDENTS

Dosan Ahn Chang Ho's life in the United States involved Korean independence activities and the founding of the first organized Korean American settlement. Korean nationalism was the focal point of his life as well as the lives of Koreans living in America. Dosan's Korean nationalism and his republican idealism paved the road to Pachappa Camp as the settlement he founded was known. The story of how this first Koreatown USA came to be, involves a citrus farm owner, a church, and some old barracks once occupied by Chinese American railroad workers.

The story of Pachappa Camp begins in March 1904, when a friend of Dosan invited him to Riverside, California. At the time, the inland county of Riverside was rich with citrus farming and the city of Riverside was considered one of the wealthiest regions in the United States. Dosan saw an opportunity for work and decided to take up his friend's invitation and move to the citrus town. On March 23, 1904, Dosan arrived in the city of Riverside, found work as a house laborer, and later as a citrus picker at Alta-Cresta Groves. While working in the groves, Dosan impressed the farm's owner, Cornelius Earle Rumsey.[35] The two influential men became

---

[35] Moses, Vincent. "Oranges and Independence: Ahn Chang Ho and Cornelius Earle Rumsey, An Early East-West Alliance in Riverside, 1904-1911." Riverside Metropolitan Museum, Riverside, California. Accessed April 5, 2006.

comrades, and their friendship would become the catalyst for the growth of the Korean American community in Riverside.

When Dosan first set foot in Riverside, he saw a disorganized group of Korean Americans trying to get jobs on citrus farms. At the time, Japanese American workers monopolized labor contracts. Thus, many Korean Americans found it difficult to find work. Dosan decided that his community needed a labor bureau. That's when Rumsey, a church member at the local Calvary Presbyterian Church, lent a helping hand. Dosan borrowed $1,500 from Rumsey to start a Korean Labor Bureau (KLB) and rent a dormitory building.[36] With the establishment of the KLB, Korean Americans could easily find work. At the same time, Rumsey also decided to hire Korean Americans as laborers on his farm and helped find housing for some of them.[37] The Korean community paid Rumsey back for his financial support in about one month.

Ahn Chang Ho, Kap Suk Cho and other workers at a Riverside orange orchard in the early 1900s. Image courtesy of the Korean American Digital Archive, Digital Library, USC.

---

[36] Ibid.

[37] Ibid.

In April 1905, the Korean Labor Bureau, which was also identified as the Korean Employment Bureau by locals, operated from 127 Cottage Street (today 3065 Cottage Street) in Riverside, but by November of the same year, the KLB had moved into a larger building across the street at 1532 Pachappa Avenue.[38] The bureau became a beacon for Korean Americans looking for work. Those who came to Riverside were also Christian, and many of them attended the local Calvary Presbyterian Church on Fourteenth Street.[39] The labor bureau became the foundation for the establishment of the first organized-Korean American settlement, or Koreatown: Pachappa Camp. Dosan founded the settlement at 1532 Pachappa Avenue, Riverside, California, near the labor bureau, possibly sometime in late 1904 or early 1905.[40] (Today, the address of the former settlement is 3096 Cottage Street).

Originally, the site was constructed for Chinese workers who built the Santa Fe Railroad in the 1880s. According to a 1905 Sanborn Insurance Map, the "Korean Settlement"—as it was named on the map—consisted of approximately twenty dwellings, vernacular, single-story, wood-frame structures, along with a one-and-a-half-story community center duplex. The wooden buildings were largely rectangular. Three were square, and another followed a rough L-plan. Each had at least one window opening. Five of the structures had awnings, twelve possessed tile chimneys, while two had stove pipes and two others had no chimneys. The insurance map labeled the structures "shanties," attesting to their poor condition.[41] The houses were drafty, as the boards that made up the wooden buildings shrank over time. One Korean resident, Mary Paik Lee, recalled putting clay in the cracks to help keep out the wind.

The homes were not equipped with gas, water, or electricity, and residents relied on outdoor water pumps and outhouses for plumbing.[42]

[38] *Riverside Enterprise,* April 20, 1905; *Riverside Daily Press,* November 10, 1905, 8.
[39] Session of Minutes. Calvary Presbyterian Church.
[40] The settlement was likely founded in 1904. Census records, church records, and *Sinhan Minbo* Korean newspaper articles, indicate that the Korean community at Pachappa Camp was already established sometime in late 1904. By 1905, there is clear evidence of the settlement's existence in newspapers and church records.
[41] *Insurance Map of Riverside, CA.* New York: Sanborn Map Company, 1908. 48.
[42] Lee, Mary Paik. *Quiet Odyssey: A Pioneer Korean Woman in America.* Seattle: University of Washington Press, 1990. 15.

The structures were painted red brick. The settlement was unique in that it was a family-based community, organized, and operated by Korean immigrants. Unlike labor camps, this first Koreatown consisted of men, women, and children and had strong activities based on family and cultural identity. Pachappa Camp was also governed by the Korean residents and was not part of a plantation or other farm, thus making it the first organized Koreatown.

Pachappa Camp residents pose in a photograph; undated photo. The settlement existed from 1904-1918. This photo was possibly taken between 1911-1913.

The local Calvary Presbyterian Church played an instrumental role in the lives of the Korean residents at Pachappa Camp. Many Koreans were Christian converts, and they came to Riverside with letters from the churches they attended in Korea:

> The following Koreans now in Riverside were certified to be members of Dr Moffat's church in Ping (Pyong) Yang, Korea; said certificate was made by Dr. Moffat personally; and on said certificate and recommendation they were admitted into full communion with this church. Their names are as follows; Lee Chi Wan: Yoon Gen Oh: Chun Nak Chung: Chun Hak Pong: Cho Chung Chul; Kim

Yoon Kak; Kim Chong Huk; Cha Eui Suk; Cha Chung Suk; Mrs Ko Chong Seen; Lee Doo Sung; Chung Dung Lup; Oh Dai Young; Kim Young Eil; Oh Chang Kon; Mrs. Lee Yul Sen; and Chun Nak Won.[43]

As the Korean community at Pachappa grew, Dosan organized it into a self-governing society. In 1905, the same year that Japan declared Korea a protectorate and began its occupation, Ahn and other community leaders such as Yi Kang established the Gongnip Hyophoe (Cooperative Association) with support from Riverside residents; the headquarters was established in San Francisco. The association's purpose was to develop democratic policies and institutions with the ultimate goal of founding a democratic Korean nation.[44] The association created a policing system, required residents to turn off their lights at nine o'clock at night, prohibited Korean women from smoking long pipes in the street, and enforced a dress code, forbidding anyone from going outside in an undershirt and encouraging the donning of a white shirt when possible.[45] According to a report by the Korean newspaper, the *Sinhan Minbo*, there were 70 Gongnip Hyophoe members in Riverside in 1905 and 150 by 1907.[46]

In 1905, Korean residents at Pachappa, with the blessing and guidance of the Calvary Presbyterian Church of Riverside, established a mission at the site.[47] The Korean mission provided English classes and church services to its members. Korean women also worked with the Women's Missionary Society at Calvary Presbyterian, visiting the camp and inviting other Korean women to the church. The two groups routinely exchanged stories and cultural knowledge. Dosan, who saw the importance of building relationships and bridges with the surrounding community, wrote the Women's Missionary Society a letter. "Mrs. Irvine also read some

---

[43] "Minutes of Session record." Calvary Presbyterian Church. December 4, 1906. Page 38.

[44] Moses, Vince. "Dosan Ahn Chang Ho: An American Pioneer." 2000.

[45] Kim, Hyung-chan. *Tosan Ahn Ch'ang-Ho: A Profile of a Prophetic Patriot*. Daegu, South Korea: Academia Koreana, Keimyung University, 1996. 35.

[46] *Sinhan Minbo*, December 11, 1905 and June 7, 1907.

[47] *Riverside Daily Press*, Riverside, California. December 7, 1905.

extracts from a letter from Mr. Ann [sic] one of the Koreans who came to Riverside."[48]

By 1907, there were more than 200 Korean residents at Pachappa Camp and between fifty and sixty attended church services. Residents at the settlement held weddings, and baptized their children, held meetings, and worked the citrus fields. The *Riverside Enterprise* newspaper noted in an article:

> The Korean mission ... has only been established a year, but is a strong organization. A majority of the members are converts from the mission in Korea. There are between fifty and sixty members. Boys from the mission attend the Calvary [C]hurch regularly. Young people from the mother church spend almost every evening teaching the young Koreans how to read and speak the English language.[49]

At the settlement, Koreans fostered a strong sense of community through their shared lifestyles. Though men worked on the farms, women also participated in the everyday functions of the camp, cooking and cleaning, maintaining their homes, and supporting their husbands. Paik Sin Koo, a Korean woman living at Pachappa, built a mud-and-straw oven to help her community; she used the oven to cook meals for several families. Another Pachappa resident, Son Kuang Do, worked tirelessly to feed the workers and cooked three meals every day for the Korean men who labored in the fields.[50] When they weren't cooking or cleaning at the settlement, Korean women went to work at local packinghouses during the harvest, helping to pack boxes with oranges, lemons, and grapefruit, which would later be shipped to stores and other businesses. The women also participated in Korean independence activities, thus taking on multiple

---

[48] *Women's Missionary Society Minutes, March 1902-October 1909.* December 10, 1906. Page 121. Note the spelling of Ahn's name is Ann. Often, Ahn Chang Ho's name was spelled as Ann, An, or Ahn.

[49] *Riverside Enterprise,* Riverside, California. December 8, 1907. Section Four, Pages 23-30.

[50] Lee, Mary Paik. *Quiet Odyssey: A Pioneer Korean Woman in America.* Seattle: University of Washington Press, 1990. 14.

duties as wives, mothers, workers, and homemakers. Koreans who didn't work on the citrus farms ended up as domestic laborers for wealthy families in the area. Some Koreans also worked at hotels, including what is now the Mission Inn in Riverside, and hospitals, as well as other local shops.[51]

By 1908, the community at Pachappa Camp numbered more than 200 residents and included men, women, and children. The families worked hard and gave much of their free time and portions of their salaries to the Korean independence movement. The money they donated went to associations like the Gongnip Hyophoe, other independence funds, and back to Korea to help alleviate the famine that was ravaging the country at the time.[52] Pachappa Camp residents gathered at the community hall and discussed plans, policies, and philosophies regarding the liberation of their motherland.

While Dosan traveled throughout America and around the world working for Korea's independence, his wife stayed in Riverside. Although Mrs. Helen Ahn gave birth to their first son Philip in Highland Park, Los Angeles, Dosan's family was living in Riverside. Dosan encouraged many Korean Americans to contribute their time, money, and minds to the cause. In 1909, Dosan and other Koreans founded the Korean National Association (KNA). Members of the Riverside Chapter of the Gongnip Hyophoe encouraged Dosan to relocate to San Francisco and establish the headquarters of the KNA there. The reason they wanted him to go there was so that the KNA could provide employment opportunities and transportation for Koreans newly arriving in San Francisco. In fact, the KNA even provided train fare and lunch boxes for newly arriving Koreans that they sent to Riverside for work, according to the Korean newspaper, the *Sinhan Minbo*. The KNA also informed the train conductor the name of the station where the Koreans should disembark.

The KNA was formed with the merging of the Gongnip Hyophoe (Cooperative Association) and the Hapsong Hyophoe (United Korean Society in Hawaii). The Korean National Association of North America

---

[51] Lee, Mary Paik. *Quiet Odyssey: A Pioneer Korean Woman in America*. Seattle: University of Washington Press, 1990; Charr, Easurk. *The Golden Mountain: The Autobiography of a Korean Immigrant, 1895–1960*. Champaign, Illinois: University of Illinois Press, 1996.

[52] *Sinhan Minbo*. May 5, 1909.

became the voice of Korean Americans, and chapters of the KNA were founded all over the Unite States. When Dosan returned to Riverside in 1911 from Korea, the KNA was reinvigorated by his vision and leadership to become a strong and cohesive group. In fact, the KNA held its third annual meeting at Pachappa Camp in 1911, and all chapter presidents, excluding the one from Mexico, attended the meeting for the first time. The *Sinhan Minbo* reported on the meeting:

> The North American KNA conference was held on November 23, 1911 in Riverside and began at 2 PM. The delegates wanted to discuss for 11 more days the 21 articles they later approved. They finalized the 21 articles and the meeting officially ended on December 4, 1911 at 3 AM. The president of North America KNA, Choi Jung-ik, attended the meeting. All nine local chapter presidents attended the meeting for the first time.[53]

Riverside community members and residents of
Pachappa Camp pose for a photo in 1911.

Although, Dosan called Riverside his place of residence from 1904 to

---

[53] *Sinhan Minbo.* December 11, 1911.

1907, he was often away because of his work for the Korean independence movement. In 1907, he went back to Korea and remained there until 1911. In September 1911, he returned to the U.S. via New York, San Francisco, and Los Angeles. He eventually made his way back to Pachappa Camp in Riverside and stayed there until 1913. However, he continued to travel extensively. Dosan's wife and children lived at Pachappa Camp from 1904 to 1913. Helen Ahn often visited neighboring towns including Claremont for work. Meanwhile, "Dosan's Republic," as Kang Myeong-hwa, who came to Riverside for the 1911 conference of the KNA of North America described it,[54] flourished. At its height, Pachappa was home to more than 300 Korean Americans.

The Hemet Valley Incident

Pachappa Camp would continue to grow until January 1913, when the "Great Freeze" decimated citrus crops in California. Job opportunities dwindled, and Koreans began looking for opportunities elsewhere. In June 1913, 11 Korean laborers from Riverside found work in nearby Hemet. The harvest was so large that year, that the ranchers feared losing part of it due to a shortage of labor. Thus, owners Joseph Simpson and William Wilson hired the Koreans for extra help picking apricots. However, anti-Japanese and anti-Asian sentiment were high at the time. White laborers confronted the 11 Koreans from Riverside at the train depot and threatened them.[55] Fearing for their lives, the Koreans left.

The Hemet Valley Incident nearly triggered an international crisis between Japan and the United States. Korea had become a protectorate of Japan in 1905 and was formally colonized in 1910, thereby making all Koreans Japanese subjects. Those Koreans living in America prior to the colonization and formal occupation of their homeland argued that they

---

[54] During the conference, delegates elected Kang president of the KNA. Moses, Vincent. "Oranges and Independence: Ahn Chang Ho and Cornelius Earle Rumsey, An Early East-West Alliance in Riverside, 1904-1911." Riverside Metropolitan Museum, Riverside, California. Accessed April 5, 2006; Patterson, Wayne, and Hyung-chan Kim. *The Koreans in America.* Minneapolis: Lerner Publishing Group, 1993. 19.

[55] *Hemet News,* Hemet, California. July 11, 1913.

were not Japanese citizens, and thus should not be treated as such. But the distinction didn't matter. The *Sinhan Minbo* reported that the white workers were anti-Asian in general and not just against the Japanese.[56] Several English and Korean newspapers reported this event and the facts were disputed. The papers provided conflicting numbers regarding the Korean workers tallying them at 11, 15, or 30. The newspapers also varied on the location from whence the Korean laborers came: Redlands, Los Angeles or Riverside. However, the *Sinhan Minbo* (July 4, 1913) reported that "eleven Korean workers from Riverside came to Hemet to work." The Korean newspaper, it's safe to say, likely provided a more accurate account as it was able to obtain the information directly from the Korean laborers.

When the Hemet Valley Incident occurred in late June 1913, the Japanese Association of Southern California tried to urge the consul general of San Francisco to consider the matter.[57] The association believed that the Koreans were "Japanese subjects." However, the Koreans involved in the incident refused Japanese assistance on their behalf, saying that this was a Korean issue.[58] U.S. Secretary of State William Jennings Bryan ordered an investigation into the problem. Bryan worried that the incident would strain U.S. – Japan relations, which were already rigid because of the 1913 California Alien Land Law. The law prohibited "aliens ineligible for citizenship" – mainly effecting Asian Americans – from owning or leasing agricultural land for long periods of time and only allowed three-year leases.

The tense diplomatic relations between the United States and Japan presented the Korean National Association with an opportunity. David Lee, the president of the KNA at the time, sent a telegram to Bryan. Lee declared to Bryan that the Hemet Valley Incident had been resolved and requested that the U.S. government cease its dealings with the Japanese government regarding Koreans in America, arguing that Koreans in the U.S. were not Japanese subjects. Bryan used Lee's declaration to alleviate the situation and published a press release stating that the Hemet incident

---

[56] *Sinhan Minbo*. July 4, 1913.

[57] "Hemet Mayor Worried: Disclaim Responsibility." *Los Angeles Times*, Los Angeles, California. June 8, 1913. Page 4.

[58] "Koreans Not Friend with the Japanese." *The Hemet News,* Hemet, California. July 11, 1913.

had been settled.[59] Bryan's press release created a *de facto* recognition of Koreans in America not as Japanese subjects, but rather as Korean nationals. Bryan's press release essentially gave Koreans in America autonomy from Japan. Thus, Korean immigrants who landed in San Francisco were able to land because they were treated as people without a country; they were considered political refugees.

Although the Hemet Valley Incident had been settled, Koreans in Riverside continued to look elsewhere for jobs. Many moved to places like Los Angeles, Dinuba, Reedley, and Willows, California and some went to other states. By 1918, the population of Pachappa Camp had dwindled to less than a handful of families and ceased to be an organized settlement.

Armed Resistance for the Korean Independence Movement

Koreans all over the United States contributed to the independence movement. One Korean American, Jang In-hwan, would make headlines for his actions against Durham White Stevens, a confidential advisor and counsel for the Japanese delegation in Washington. Stevens' public statements about Koreans living better lives under Japanese rule had outraged Jang and his fellow Korean nationals in San Francisco. Korean representatives met with Stevens and asked him to issue an apology statement, but he refused, angering the Korean representatives who threw chairs at Stevens and created a scene on March 22, 1908. One day later, on March 23, 1908, Jang In-hwan shot and killed Durham White Stevens (1851-1908) in San Francisco. Jang was arrested and sentenced to 25 years in prison. The incident captured headlines. Newspapers, including the *Los Angeles Herald*, reported the story.

In the early 1900s, Dosan and other Koreans like Philip Jaisohn, Park Yong-man, and Syngman Rhee worked tirelessly for the independence of their homeland. Park Yong-man was a notable Korean American and a "sworn brother" of Syngman Rhee. The pair were arrested by pro-Japanese law enforcement and imprisoned in Korea. Park emigrated to the United States after his release. He obtained a student visa and enrolled in the

---

[59] "Hemet's Korean Incident Closed by Bryan's Order." *San Francisco Call*, San Francisco, California. July 2, 1913.

University of Nebraska in 1908. One year later, in June 1909, Park established a military school on a farm about one mile west of the Buffalo County Court House in Hastings, Nebraska.

The Korean Youth Military Academy started with 13 cadets. Much like a military academy, the students learned infantry strategy, other soldierly duties, as well as English, mathematics, and science. From 9 AM to 6:30 PM, the Korean cadets trained and studied.[60] Supported by the Korean National Association, the school grew, and by 1910, 26 students enrolled for its summer program. The students practiced military drills and trained to fight against Japan. However, by 1914, the students left the area for other locations, and the school ceased operations. Yet, Park's academy was able to graduate 100 Korean reserve officers for the independence movement. Several years later – during the 1920s and 1930s – many of those men enlisted in the Korean Independence Army.[61] The school's example inspired others, and like-minded facilities were set up all over the United States including in Oahu, Hawaii; Lompoc, California; and Kansas City and Superior, Wyoming. One was even established in Mérida, Mexico.

Park Yong-man in military uniform in 1910.

---

[60] *The Kearney Daily Hub*. Kearney, Nebraska. August 30, 1909.
[61] Park Young. *Korea and the Imperialists: In Search of National Identity*. Bloomington, Indiana: AuthorHouse, 2009. 142.

Korean American Highlight
Dosan Ahn Chang Ho

Portrait photograph of Dosan Ahn Chang Ho.
Image courtesy of the Korean American Digital Archive, Digital Library, USC.

Ahn Chang Ho was born on November 9, 1878, in Kangseo, Pyeongan Province, in what is now North Korea. He often went by his pen name, Dosan, which means "island mountain." His life is characterized as one of sacrifice, honor, and distinction. His father died when he was just eight years old.[62] Dosan continued his traditional Chinese studies until he was sixteen. In 1894, he traveled to Seoul, where he studied at the Miller Academy, learning English and converting to Christianity. In 1897, Dosan joined Philip Jaisohn's Independence Association. The next year, he gave a speech at the Pan-National Coalition Conference, where he distinguished himself as an excellent speaker.

Dosan's commitment to learning motivated him to establish the progressive Cheonjin Hakkyo, or Gradual Progress School, in Tongjin,

---

[62] Kim, Hyung-chan. *Tosan Ahn Ch'ang-ho: A Profile of a Prophetic Patriot*. Seoul: Tosan Memorial Foundation, 1996. 13.

Gangseo County in Korea.[63] In 1902, Dosan married Lee Hye-ryon (Helen). Together, they were the first Korean couple to immigrate to the United States.[64] Dosan hoped to study education, western values, and democratic ideals in America. However, Dosan and his wife boarded the wrong ship from Hawaii and ended up in Vancouver, Canada, before finally arriving in San Francisco on October 14, 1902. While wandering the streets of San Francisco, Dosan ran into Dr. Drew, a former Korean missionary, who took the young couple in and helped them.[65]

In 1903, Dosan established the Chinmoke Hoe (Friendship Society) in San Francisco. Dosan worked as a houseboy and later made his way to Riverside, California, at the suggestion of his friend who was already living in the citrus-rich community. Dosan arrived in Riverside on March 23, 1904. He established a Korean Labor Bureau and later the first organized Korean American settlement – Pachappa Camp – at 1532 Pachappa Avenue in Riverside. The community flourished from 1905 to 1913, and at its height, families and workers residing in the camp numbered around 300. (The community eventually dwindled out of existence and by 1918, Pachappa Camp ceased operations). He also founded the Gongnip Hyophoe (Cooperative Association) in 1905. On March 29 of that same year, Dosan's oldest son, Philip was born.

In 1906, Dosan and his fellow Korean immigrants at Pachappa Camp started plans to initiate the New Korea Society. However, Dosan left the United States in 1907 to continue his independence activities, and the New Korea Society (Shinminhoe) was founded in Korea that year. Dosan worked hard against Japanese occupation and influence in Korea. In 1909, he was accused and arrested for conspiring to assassinate a Japanese official. Cleared of the charges, he was released after two months. Later, he was elected the president of the Korean National Association of North America (KNA), which he helped found in San Francisco in 1909. The KNA was dedicated to the independence of Korea. The KNA played an important role in the lives of Korean Americans and of Koreans worldwide.

---

[63] Ibid., page 26.

[64] "Ahn Chang Ho." *New World Encyclopedia*. October 27, 2016. http://www.new-worldencyclopedia.org/entry/Ahn_Chang_Ho.

[65] "Corea the Sleeping Land: Its Queer People. Strange Customs and Coming Awakening." *San Francisco Chronicle*, December 7, 1902.

In 1910, Ahn went to China to promote the Korean independence movement, and in 1911, he went to Russia, Manchuria, and England, before eventually finding his way back to the United States. In 1911, the Korean National Association of North America held its third national convention at Pachappa Camp, which was hailed as a success by Korean newspapers. The convention gathered every chapter president of the KNA – except for the one in Mexico – in Riverside, California. Dosan was welcomed back to the United States during the conference. One year later, in 1912, Dosan's second son – Philson – was born in Riverside.

In 1913, Dosan organized and established the Heung Sa Dan (Young Korean Academy) in San Francisco. Dosan's family left Riverside in December 1913 and moved to Los Angeles. They lived at several locations including a location that became the Ahn Family House, which still stands today on the University of Southern California campus.

For years, Dosan traveled and worked for his homeland's freedom. He often went back and forth from the United States to Mexico, China, Korea, and Russia. In Los Angeles, Helen Ahn gave birth to their daughter, Susan, in 1915. In 1917, Soorah, Dosan's fourth child and second daughter was born in Los Angeles. In 1919, Dosan traveled to Shanghai, China, where he helped to establish and lead the Korean Provisional Government. Here Dosan wrote many speeches, articles, and books on Korean society, independence, and education.

In 1924, Dosan finally returned to the United States for a lengthy stay after working in China for the Korean Provisional Government in Shanghai, establishing schools and writing papers. In the United States, he continued his work for Korea's independence. However, in 1926, after being falsely accused of being a Bolshevist, he was deported to Australia, from there he made his way back to Shanghai, China. Meanwhile, his wife Helen gave birth to their youngest child, Philander "Ralph," in the United States. While in China, Dosan became a naturalized citizen. He continued to work for Korean independence by writing articles, speeches, and more.

For years, Dosan worked to establish branches of the Korean National Association around the world, including one in the Philippines. However, in 1932, Dosan was falsely accused of being connected to a bombing implemented by Korean independence activist Yun Bong-gil at Hongkew Park in China. The incident killed several Japanese dignitaries. Japanese authorities arrested Dosan and illegally extradited him to Korea. After years of being in exile, Dosan finally returned to his homeland. However, Dosan's return was marked with tribulations; he was put on trial and convicted, sent to Taejon prison, tortured, and kept under heavy guard. Dosan's health declined rapidly during his imprisonment. Japanese authorities feared he would die and released him. He was sent to Seoul National University Hospital where he died in March 1938, a Korean martyr. Dosan was honored by the South Korean government for his independence work and was posthumously awarded the Presidential Medal in 1962. In 1969, Helen Ahn died in Los Angeles. Today, Ahn Chang Ho and Helen are buried at Dosan Park in South Korea.[66]

In 2001, the City of Riverside erected a statue of Dosan to honor his work, his vision, and to remember the Korean community that lived, worked, and died in the area. Funds for the statue were raised by the Dosan Ahn Chang Ho Memorial Foundation of America in Riverside. Dr. Myung Ki "Mike" Hong led the effort and was president of the foundation at the time. In December 2016, the City of Riverside also designated the site of Pachappa Camp as its first point of cultural interest, honoring Dosan's legacy and the first Koreatown, USA.[67] A dedication was held on March 23, 2017, and Dosan's youngest son, Ralph Ahn, attended the ceremony with his wife, Ann.

---

[66] Kim, Hyung-chan. *Tosan Ahn Ch'ang-ho: A Profile of a Prophetic Patriot.* Seoul: Tosan Memorial Foundation, 1996: 249-270.

[67] Constante, Agnes. "California City Honors First Korean Settlement in U.S." *NBC News*, March 24, 2017. https://www.nbcnews.com/news/asian-america/california-city-honors-first-korean-settlement-u-s-n738321. Accessed September 18, 2018.

Korean American Highlight
Soon Hak Kim

Soon Hak Kim's headstone still stands at Evergreen
Cemetery in Riverside, California.

Born in 1876 in Korea, Soon Hak Kim was a pioneering Korean American who lived and died in Riverside, California. He worked at the Riverside Glenwood Hotel, later the Mission Inn, as a baker. While in Riverside, he became an integral part of Pachappa Camp, the first organized Korean American settlement. A religious man, he was the pastor of the Korean mission established by the local Calvary Presbyterian Church at Pachappa Camp.

Kim worked diligently for the Korean independence movement. Tragically, Kim died in a buggy accident in 1919. The story was reported by the *Riverside Enterprise* newspaper. He is buried at Evergreen Cemetery in Riverside where his tombstone reads, "Soon Hak Kim, member of Korean

National Association and Young Korean Academy." Soon Hak Kim's son, Joseph Kim (Tae Sun Kim), also died tragically at a young age from cancer. His son is also buried at Evergreen Cemetery in Riverside, California.

Korean American Highlight
Violet Catherine Kim

Portrait of Catherine Violet Kim as a young woman.

Violet Catherine Kim was born on November 22, 1922, in Riverside, California. She was the daughter of Yong Ryon Kim and Hazel Han Kim. Violet went by the name Catherine and had five siblings: Samson, Mallie, Mae, Lucy, and John. Catherine's grandfather, In Soo Kim, was a distant relative of Dosan Ahn Chang Ho's wife, Helen Ahn. In Soo Kim played an important role in shaping the daily lives of the Koreans at Pachappa Camp. He worked as a labor contractor at the Korean Labor Bureau and served as the Riverside chapter president of the Gongnip Hyophoe.

Catherine attended Riverside Polytechnic High School and earned a degree from the University of California Los Angeles (UCLA). Catherine's family had a small farm in Riverside and a 30-acre vineyard in Delano, which was started by In Soo Kim in either 1912 or 1913. Catherine worked as a laborer at the March Field Air Base in Riverside as a general mechanic helper and junior mechanic in 1942 and 1943.

In September 1959, Catherine became a teacher at the Grand Terrace, Terrace View, and Lincoln Schools for the Colton Joint School Districts. She retired in June 1984. Catherine's long history of community involvement and leadership includes her friendship with the Inabas, a Japanese American family. The friendship was rare at the time, given that Koreans and Japanese did not get along, even after Korea regained independence in 1945. The Kim and Inaba families met at the Yamada Wholesale Market in Riverside just before World War II. Catherine and Mallie Kim often picked strawberries at the Inaba family's farm in Riverside. The two families formed a lifelong friendship; they shared the crops they grew, made jams and cookies, and even helped the Inabas host "Mochitsuki," an annual tradition in which rice is pounded to be made into *mochi*. Meiko Inaba and her husband, Mitz Inaba, helped Catherine and her sister Mallie operate their small farm in Riverside. The families visited each other often, demonstrating that friendships and kindness surpass ethnic and cultural prejudices and boundaries.

Catherine died in April 2018 and was buried near her parents at Olivewood Cemetery in Riverside, California.[68]

---

[68] Information about Catherine was provided by her family in April 2018. A eulogy document was donated to the YOK Center containing a summary of Catherine's life.

CHAPTER 3

THE KOREAN INDEPENDENCE MOVEMENT

World War I, Origins of the Korean Air Force, and the Role of the Church

The outbreak of World War I on July 28, 1914, changed the Korean American community forever. Many Korean Americans enlisted in the U.S. military and served with honor and valor. The *New Korea* reported on these brave young men including: Kim Yong-song, Kim Jung-eun, Lee Sang-ku, and Park Han-ku.[69] Edward Surk Cho Lee became the highest ranking Korean American in the U.S. Army during World War I. He earned the rank of sergeant and became the first soldier of Korean nationality to become a naturalized U.S. citizen.[70] Meanwhile, with the support of the Korean National Association, Park Yong-man moved to Hawaii where he planned to continue his military training and efforts for the Korean independence movement. He consolidated all the Korean American military units in the United States in Ahuimanu, Oahu, Hawaii. Thus, on August 29, 1914, the consolidated forces became the Korean National Brigade or the Dae Hanin Kuk Min Koon Dan.[71]

Another extraordinary Korean American was George Lee (Lee

---

[69] *New Korea*. August 9, 1917.

[70] Chang, Roberta, and Patterson, Wayne. *The Koreans in Hawaii: A Pictorial History 1903-2003*. Honolulu: University of Hawaii Press, 2003. Page 95.

[71] Ibid., pages 72-73.

Eng-hyo). He enlisted in the U.S. military sometime in late 1917 and became the first pilot of Korean origin. Lee was born in Chemulpo (Incheon), Korea in 1896. He migrated to the U.S. in early 1903 and worked with his father on a sugar beet farm in Hawaii. He flew on more than 156 missions in blimps and other airships during World War I.[72] George Lee should be recognized as the first Korean pilot in history.

The fledgling aviation industry took off during World War I and would inspire the Korean American community. When the conflict ended on November 11, 1918, Korean Americans found themselves living all over the United States. Many were living and working in Northern California farm towns like Reedley, Dinuba, and Willows. One Korean American – Kim Chong-lim – became a millionaire. The "Rice King." as he was nicknamed, made his fortune during the war, when demand for rice skyrocketed. Kim farmed in Northern California's Glenn County where from 1913 to 1920, the rice farming industry thrived. Kim began farming operations in 1914. By 1919, he farmed 3,300 acres of rice.[73] At the time he leased the land with white partners, thus circumventing the Alien Land Law of 1913, which barred any immigrant ineligible for citizenship to own or lease land for long periods of time. The law targeted Japanese immigrants and thus affected Korean Americans, whose homeland was considered a protectorate of Japan. Kim's success would later allow him to become an instrumental character in the founding of the Korean Aviation School and Corps in Willows, California.

In 1919, the March First *Mansei* protest in Korea sparked a worldwide movement and motivated Koreans to do more for the independence of their homeland. The Korean Provisional Government (KPG) was established in April of that same year and was headquartered in Shanghai, China, where General Roh Paik-lin was appointed defense minister. Meanwhile, the Korean American community, who saw themselves as Korean nationals, discussed what more they could do for their homeland and decided to establish an aviation school and train combat pilots. General Roh arrived in San Francisco and met with Kim Chong-lim, learned of the plan to open a Korean combat pilot aviation school, and joined the effort to establish the Korean American Aviation School and Corps in Willows, California.

---

[72] *Stockton Daily Record*. December 18, 1918.
[73] Chang, Edward. *Korean American Pioneer Aviators: The Willows Airmen*. Lexington Books. 2015. Pages 10-11.

Korean student pilots at the Willows Korean Aviation School
and Corps pose for a photograph in 1920. Image courtesy of the
Korean American Digital Archive, Digital Library, USC.

General Roh received endorsement and approval from the Korean Provisional Government to aid in the process of opening the combat pilot training school. With plans in place, the only remaining obstacle was to secure more funding. The Korean American community in Northern California had already gathered some support, but it wasn't enough until Kim, an avid Korean independence activist, agreed to donate $50,000, a substantial amount of money to help open the school.[74] (In 2019 currency, the funds Kim donated is equivalent to nearly two thirds of a million dollars).

Kim's passion for Korean independence followed him from his homeland. He arrived in the United States in 1907 and worked various railroad jobs before heading to California in 1908. He became a businessman and donated food, money, and time to the independence movement. In 1913, he co-founded the Young Korean Academy with Ahn Chang Ho and Cho Byung-oak. Kim's desire to help free Korea was deeply rooted and when presented the opportunity to help found an aviation school, he did.

---

[74] Ibid.

The Willows Korean Aviation School and Corps opened in March 1920 and enrolled an initial class of 24 young men.[75] Instructor Frank "Happy" Bryant oversaw flight training. Cadets trained using, according to varying accounts, the three-to-five planes the school had purchased.[76] Many of the young Korean men already had some training from the Redwood City Aviation School in Northern California.

Unfortunately, a torrential storm destroyed the Rice King's farms in October 1920, and thus, major funding for the Korean aviation school was lost. The facility officially furled its wings in July 1921. Today, the Korean Air Force recognizes the Willows Korean Aviation School and Corps as its origin. Two of the school's graduates, Park Hee-sung and Lee Yong-keun, were later appointed by the Korean Provisional Government as its first aviation officers, thus connecting Korean American, Korean, and American history.[77]

Despite the school's demise, Korean Americans continued to support the independence movement of their homeland through other activities. They held meetings, donated funds to the Korean Provisional Government in Shanghai, China, organized military schools, and trained themselves to help fight a war against Japan. During the 1920s, these Korean nationals established various organizations and associations throughout the United States. The Delta Fraternity and Sorority Club was established in 1922 and actively held and supported community events highlighting Korean culture.[78]

By the mid-to-late 1920s, the Korean American community was split when it came to political support for either Dosan Ahn Chang Ho or Syngman Rhee. The two great men apparently had a falling out in 1921,[79] furthering the division of the Korean American community's political support. Both men were leaders with different styles and approaches to gaining Korea's freedom. Rhee helped lead the Korean Provisional Government

---

[75] *New Korea*. March 1, 1920.

[76] It is unclear if the school owned three or five planes. Reports vary.

[77] Chang, Edward. *Korean American Pioneer Aviators: The Willows Airmen*. Lexington Books. 2015.

[78] Chang, Roberta, and Wayne Patterson. *The Koreans in Hawaii: A Pictorial History 1903-2003*. Honolulu: University of Hawaii Press, 2003. Pages 132-133.

[79] Ibid., Page 109.

while Dosan founded the Korean National Association, the voice of the Korean American community and Koreans all over the world. However, in 1925, Rhee was impeached[80] over allegations that he misused his power with the Korean Provisional Government.

Rhee went back to Hawaii and asked for help from the Dongji Hoe (Comrade Association), a group that was headed by one of his supporters. Rhee set up the Dongji Investment Company, but it went bankrupt after five years. Meanwhile, Dosan Ahn Chang Ho was deported from the U.S. in March 1926 after false accusations were made against him by Kong Wong and Charles Hong Lee; they sent a letter to the U.S. Immigration Office falsely accusing Ahn of being a Bolshevist.[81]

The Korean American Community in the Interwar Period

The Korean population in the United States remained stagnant in the 1920s. In California, Koreans continued to worship and establish churches and organizations. In fact, the role of the church in the Korean American community served as more than just a place of worship. Korean Americans used church as a place to conduct independence activities, provide social services, education, and at times business and familial transactions.

During the 1920s, Koreans in the United States not only founded the Willows Korean Aviation School and Corps, they also continued their lobbying efforts even though on March 17, 1920 the U.S. Senate voted down a bill to sympathize with the Korean independence movement, 34 to 46. During this decade, Koreas in America also set up businesses including trucking, grocery, and fruit nurseries. Notably, Charles Ho Kim and Harry Kim (not brothers), set up the Kim Brothers Co., and invented the nectarine in 1920.

By the 1930s, the Korean American community had put down roots. Children of the first immigrants were growing up. In Los Angeles, the

---

[80] Ibid., Page 138.
[81] U.S. Department of Labor, Immigration Service, Office of the Commissioner Angel Island Station Via Ferry Post Office, December 24, 1924. Document No. 238880/1-6. Investigation Arrival Case Files, San Francisco, Records of the U.S. Immigration and Naturalization Service, RG 85, National Archives, Pacific Region, San Bruno, California.

Korean United Presbyterian Church, which had been founded on Jefferson Boulevard in 1906, was thriving. The Korean United Methodist Church of San Francisco was built in 1928 after the Korean American community raised $18,000 to purchase the site. In Hawaii, Korean Americans continued to set up churches, including the Korean Methodist Episcopal Center.

During the 1930s, Korean Americans continued trying to convince the United States government to support the independence of their homeland. On April 20, 1933 William H. Lee and Haan Kil-su sent a forty-page "Korean's Appeal" document to the U.S. government, urging them to employ anti-Japanese Koreans for anti-Japanese activities. In 1938, the Korean National Association building was dedicated and shared the same campus as the Korean United Presbyterian Church on Jefferson Boulevard in Los Angeles. The KNA building served as a central hub for independence activities.

During this period, Koreans resided all over the United States, however many of them were living in California, though the population was still small. In Los Angeles, approximately 650 Koreans formed a community in an area that is now South-Central Los Angeles. Many Korean Americans also lived in Los Angeles' downtown Bunker Hill area, which is known as "Old Koreatown."

Korean National Association members attend the dedication of
the KNA's new building in Los Angeles on April 17, 1938.
Image courtesy of the Korean American Digital Archive, Digital Library, USC.

The Role of Churches and Christianity in the Korean American Community

Christianity and the role of the church in the Korean American community are significant. Many of the pioneering Koreans that made their way to Hawaii were Christian converts and were encouraged to leave their homeland by American missionaries. The church played an integral and important role in the lives of the early Korean immigrant community. American churches not only established missions, but also provided spiritual salvation, English classes, and at times monetary assistance for Korean immigrants. For example, Calvary Presbyterian Church in Riverside, California, provided its congregants with teachers, finances, and created a mission at Pachappa Camp in 1905.

In other places, Korean Americans established their own churches with the assistance or guidance of larger American churches. For example, in Hawaii, the Korean Methodist Church was established in 1903. The church helped Korean immigrants adapt to their plantation lives. A Korean Methodist mission in Los Angeles was established at Mrs. Sherman's home in 1904. The Korean Methodist Church of San Francisco held its first service in October 1905. The Korean Presbyterian Church was established in Los Angeles in 1906.[82] During the early 1900s, Korean Americans established churches in Hawaii, California, and various other states. Immanuel Presbyterian Church and Wilshire Christian Church were both established in the 1920s in Los Angeles.

The Korean independence movement was the main topic of discussion for Koreans in America during the early 1900s, and the church and the independence movement grew inseparable. Many Korean immigrants used church as a center to network, communicate, and work with other Koreans for the freedom of their homeland. Syngman Rhee, a Christian convert, used the church as a political vehicle. Early Korean immigrant churches practiced religious nationalism, advocated for the independence of Korea, and taught the Korean language and identity to young children.

After the end of World War II and Korea gained its freedom, Korean American church activities shifted. The post-1965 Korean immigrant

---

[82] Lee Young, Judy. *Marginality: The Key to Multicultural Theology*. Minneapolis: Augsburg Fortress Press, 1995. Page 178.

churches became more conservative, evangelical, and strong advocates of revivalism. Moreover, the focus of Korean immigrants changed to homeland politics, primarily toward the reunification of North and South Korea.

In the 1900s, only one percent of the population of Korea were Christian. By 2014, 29 percent of the South Korean population identified as Christian.[83] In the United States, Korean Americans are predominantly Christian, with 71 percent of the population identifying with the religion.[84] The Korean American population is strongly tied to its church as a central hub for religious, social, educational, and political activities. Church and the Christian faith continue to be strong influences in the Korean American community today.

The Korean Methodist Church, Los Angeles. 1950.
Image courtesy of the Korean American Digital Archive, Digital Library, USC.

---

[83] Connor, Phillip. "6 Facts About South Korea's Growing Christian Population." *Pew Research Center.* August 12, 2014. www.pewresearch.org/fact-tank/2014/08/12/6-facts-about-christianity-in-south-korea/.
[84] Ibid.

Korean American Highlight
George Lee: First Korean Pilot

Born in 1896 in Chemulpo (Incheon), Korea, George Lee immigrated to Hawaii in 1903. His Korean name was Lee Eng-hyo. Lee worked with his father on a sugar beet farm in Hawaii for two years. Over time, Lee's father, Lee Du-hyung, saved enough money to lease land in Stockton, California. However, the family struggled financially. Lee's father was a devoted Korean independence activist and donated his time and what little money he had to the movement. The family was also close to Dosan Ahn Chang Ho and supported him.

George Lee was just 18 when World War I broke out; he enlisted in the U.S. Army. His registration card described him as short and single. Lee trained to become a pilot for the U.S. military.[85] He trained for six months in Texas, was sent to South Carolina for further instruction, and graduated from aviation school in New York.[86] On June 18, 1918, he was sent overseas, and over the course of World War I, he flew 156 missions.[87] He flew near the German and French borders and piloted a blimp.[88]

After the war, Lee was honorably discharged. He lived in New York and studied electrical engineering. He married an American woman, with whom he had a son. Lee's aviation record and service during World War I make him the first Korean pilot.

Korean American Highlight
Ellen Thun

Born in Riverside, California, in 1912, Ellen Thun lived at Pachappa Camp, went to grammar school in the city, and later went to high school and college in Los Angeles.[89] Thun worked as a proofreader at the *Times-Mirror Press* in Los Angeles and married Cyril Zimmerman. She was the

---

[85] *New Korea*, May 24, 1918.

[86] *Stockton Daily Record*, December 18, 1918.

[87] Ibid.

[88] *New Korea*, December 26, 1918.

[89] Thun, Ellen. "Immigrants: Mainstream, USA." *The Korea Times*. January 8, 2001. www.koreatimes.com/ article/20817.

cousin of Jacob Dunn, a prominent Korean American leader who also lived and worked in Riverside for a period.

Ellen Thun and her brother Sam Thun in 1943.
Photo courtesy of Ellen Thun.

Ellen's family was large. Her parents Nak Chung Thun and Young Soon "Ruth" Thun had seven children: Obed Thun (1906), Samson Thun (1908), Elizabeth (1910), Ellen Thun (1912), Jack Thun (1914), Amos Thun, and Arthur Thun (1918).

Ellen Thun's early life was riddled with tragedy and hardship while she lived in Riverside. Her mother, "Ruth," committed suicide and her father became estranged from her brothers. Ellen Thun also had a stillborn twin sister. For a time, Ellen Thun and her brothers were sent to an orphanage, following their mother's death. However, despite the issues and problems, Ellen Thun and her siblings grew up to become successful and happy.[90]

Ellen Thun became a prolific writer and authored "Heart Warmers," a series of columns that ran in the *Korea Times* newspaper. She spent her life helping to document Korean American history through her articles and writings and died in 2006.[91]

---

[90] Interview with Ellen Thun by Edward T. Chang on February 23, 1993 at her apartment in Los Angeles. Interview with Ellen Thun by Edward T. Chang in Riverside on July 1, 1992.

[91] Ibid.

CHAPTER 4

WORLD WAR II, KOREAN AMERICAN HEROES, AND THE KOREAN WAR

On September 1, 1939, Germany invaded Poland, and World War II broke out. The United States remained outside of the conflict until the bombing of Pearl Harbor by Japan on December 7, 1941, which effectively opened the Pacific Theater. (The bombing also served as the impetus for Japanese American internment. In 1942, under Executive Order 9066, between 110,000 – 120,000 Japanese Americans were interned in concentration camps in the United States).

Meanwhile, Korean Americans, motivated by nationalism for both their countries, heeded this call to action and enlisted in the U.S. military. Three of Ahn Chang Ho's children joined at this time: Philip Ahn, who had already started his career as an actor, enlisted in the U.S. Army; Susan Ahn became the first female gunnery officer in the U.S. Navy; and Ralph Ahn, Dosan's youngest son, also enlisted in the U.S. Navy. John Park was killed in action during the storming of Normandy on D-Day. Fred Ohr became a flying ace for the U.S. Air Force. In Los Angeles, more than one hundred Korean Americans joined the California National Guard and formed the "Tiger Brigade."

Korean unit of the California National Guard in front of Los Angeles City Hall. Image courtesy of the Korean American Digital Archive, Digital Library, USC.

One of the most famous Korean Americans to serve in the U.S. military was Young Oak Kim. He enlisted during World War II and became an officer of the U.S. Army. His valor and bravery during World War II captured newspaper headlines including the *Los Angeles Times*. In fact, Kim was well known for his leadership of the 100th Battalion/442nd Regimental Combat Team, also known as the Nisei Unit. Kim was assigned to this mostly Japanese American unit in Hawaii. When he arrived, his commanding officer wanted to transfer him because Koreans and Japanese didn't get along at the time, but Kim refused saying, "Sir, they're Americans, and I'm an American. We're going to fight for America, so I want to stay."[92]

Kim trained with the unit in Hawaii, and in 1943 the 100th Infantry Battalion received its first assignment in North Africa. Later, the unit headed to Italy. Kim's bravery at the Battle of Anzio in Italy is legendary. Kim and one of his men, Irving Akahoshi, crawled through a minefield,

---

[92] Han, Woo Sung and Edward T. Chang. *Unsung Hero: The Story of Col. Young Oak Kim*. Riverside, California: Young Oak Kim Center, University of California Riverside Press, 2011. Page 30.

captured two German soldiers, and made their way back across the line. The information gathered from the German prisoners of war (POWs) helped the Allied Forces push forward. Kim was promoted to the rank of captain for his actions. He also earned recognition for liberating Rome and for his actions during the liberation of Pisa. Later, Kim was wounded in Biffontaine, France.

Kim's military prowess was due in part to his unique talent for visualizing maps in three dimensions. Kim earned the respect of many of his superior officers who valued his abilities. Kim and the 100th/442nd RCT would earn countless medals and honors for their actions. The unit's motto, "Go for Broke," became famous; the 442nd Regimental Combat Team is the most decorated unit for its size and length of service in U.S. military history. The 18,000 men in the unit earned 9,486 Purple Hearts, 21 Medals of Honor, and 7 Presidential Citations. Unfortunately, Col. Young Oak Kim was not one of the 21 recipients of the Medal of Honor.

Korean Americans fought bravely during World War II and saw it as their way of contributing to the U.S. fight against Japan and the liberation of Korea. In fact, more than 200 Korean Americans from the U.S. mainland and several hundred additional troops from Hawaii enlisted in the U.S. Army, Navy, and Air Force during the war. Korean Americans enlisted because they believed their service was a way to contribute to the independence of their homeland. Richard Shinn was one of these brave and notable Korean Americans who fought during World War II. Shinn was part of the 101st Airborne Division, and he fought in the Battle of the Bulge. Shinn was wounded in action by shrapnel from a hand grenade, for which he received a Purple Heart. After the war, Shinn became a successful professional boxer. He settled down in his hometown of San Francisco where he raised his family.

Korean American Identity after World War II

When World War II ended on September 2, 1945 with the surrender of the Japanese forces, Korea became a free nation once more. However, the Korean peninsula would be split at the 38th parallel by the Allied Forces, with the United States taking control of the south and the Soviet

Union taking the north. In 1948, Syngman Rhee became president of the Republic of South Korea. Kim Il-sung would become the leader of the Democratic People's Republic of Korea in the north.

With Korea now a divided peninsula free of Japanese rule, Korean Americans no longer invested time in the independence movement. As a result, their nationalistic identity began to change. Many Korean Americans attended schools in the U.S. and became doctors, lawyers, engineers, and studied in multiple fields. Korean American Dr. Sammy Lee became the first Asian American man to win an Olympic gold medal for the United States in 1948 during the London Games. Born in Fresno, California, Dr. Lee moved to Los Angeles at a young age, where he was good friends with the future Col. Young Oak Kim. There, Lee's parents owned a chop suey restaurant. Dr. Lee was inspired to become a diver after seeing signs for the 1932 Olympic Games posted all over Los Angeles. Dr. Lee pursued his dream with a passion and became a champion diver.[93]

By 1947, he had earned his medical degree from the University of Southern California and continued his diving career. He trained for the next Olympic Games, yet his road to gold was paved in obstacles. Dr. Lee was limited to practicing at his local pool once a week because it was otherwise closed to minorities. The pool water was purportedly drained and refilled after the open day for minorities. Ironically, it was later discovered that the water was never drained. The pool owner claimed to drain the water only to appease his white swimmers. However, due to the minority policy, Dr. Lee was forced to train elsewhere, so his coach dug a hole in his backyard, filled it with soft dirt, and continued helping Lee practice his diving rotations. Landing in the dirt, Dr. Lee said, hurt his back.[94]

Rising above discrimination and racism, Dr. Lee won gold again at the 1952 Helsinki Olympic Games. Dr. Lee also joined the U.S. Army Medical Corps and served a tour of duty in Korea, where he attained the rank of major. Dr. Lee won several awards for his diving including the Amateur Athletic Union's James E. Sullivan Award.

---

[93] According to an interview of Dr. Sammy Lee, conducted on March 24, 2015 at his home.

[94] Ibid.

Dr. Sammy Lee holds his Sullivan Award on February 21, 1954.
Image courtesy of the Korean American Digital Archive, Digital Library, USC.

The population of Korean Americans living in the United States during the 1940s was very small, totaling approximately 9,000, but this small community of first- and second-generation Korean Americans persevered. Many Korean Americans owned restaurants and small grocery stores in areas like Los Angeles, New York, and other cities. By the end of the 1940s, Korean Americans like Dr. Sammy Lee and Young Oak Kim, helped this small community gain marginal recognition in the United States.

The Korean War

The Korean War (1950-1953), or the "Forgotten War," lasted for three years and resulted in a cease-fire; the country remained split afterwards. On June 25, 1950, 750,000 North Korean troops invaded South Korea and sparked the Korean War. The United States backed South Korea and sent American troops to aid in the conflict, believing the invasion was the start of a communist campaign that could not be left unchecked.[95] Young Oak Kim, who had been honorably discharged from the U.S. Army in 1946, reenlisted despite the objections of his friends and family. Kim wanted to fight on the frontlines in Korea, so he could do his part in uniting his parents' homeland. During the war, Kim became the first minority battalion commander during combat in U.S. Army history. He helped push past the 38th parallel on three separate occasions.

Figure 1. Map of the Korean Peninsula

Sources: Map produced by CRS using data from ESRI, and the U.S. Department of State's Office of the Geographer.

A map of the Korean peninsula depicting the 38th parallel. Image courtesy of a Congressional Research Service Report published in October 2017.

For three years, the conflict in Korea raged. The war claimed the lives of 36,574 Americans in-theater, as well as the lives of more than 1.2 million South Korean military personnel and civilians. More than 1 million North

---

[95] "Korean War." History.com Editors. A&E Television Networks. Published November 9, 2009 and updated November 10, 2018. Accessed February 22, 2019. https://www.history.com/topics/korea/korean-war.

Korean military personnel and civilians also died in the conflict. China sent troops to aid North Korea and pushed South Korean and American forces back below the 38th parallel. About 600,000 Chinese troops died during the war.[96] As the casualties mounted, a truce to the fighting was proposed in 1951. However, the peace talks would take two years, but South Korea ultimately refused to sign the agreement. Instead, the United Nations, the Democratic People's Republic of Korea, and the Chinese People's Volunteers signed the armistice on July 27, 1953.[97] The two sides would technically remain at war, even to this day. Korea is still divided at the 38th parallel with both the north and the south maintaining 2,200 yards of border spanning from this center point. The division, known as the Demilitarized Zone (DMZ), is the most heavily guarded border in the world. The DMZ also represents the separation of 10 million Korean families, most of whom have not seen each other since 1953. The Korean War and the division of the peninsula changed Korean American political activities; they now focused on homeland politics and the reunification of North and South Korea. Today, the issue is still a top priority for Koreans all over the world.

Korean War Adoptees

The aftermath of the Korean War left thousands of children orphaned or abandoned. Also, during the war, U.S. soldiers on deployment fathered unwanted children. The mixed-race children were often left at orphanages and were stigmatized in South Korea; they were seen as noncitizens without social or legal status. The adoption of Korean war orphans and unwanted mixed-race children, also known as "G.I. babies" began in the mid-1950s and can be traced back to the Holt International Children's Services organization. Founded by Harry and Bertha Holt in 1956, the faith-based company began when the couple decided to adopt eight children from South Korea in 1955. The South Korean government wanted to have its G.I. babies adopted, and when Holt proposed an organized

---

[96] "Korean War Fast Facts." CNN. June 10, 2017, http://www.cnn.com/2013/06/28/world/asia/korean-war-fast-facts/index.html.

[97] Ibid.

program, it agreed. The South Korean government revised its laws on emigration and adoption and created a child placement agency.[98] The program, which was originally created to help G.I. babies find homes, changed in the 1960s to include more full-blooded Korean children as well. Holt's program flourished, and thousands of Korean children were adopted by Americans. Since 1955, about 100,000 Korean children were adopted by American families.[99]

A North Korean Guard glares at a ROK Army Guard as they positioned themselves on either side of the Military Demarcation Line (MDL) or DMZ, prior to a repatriation ceremony at the Panmunjom Freedom House for what is believed to be five U.S. soldiers killed in the Korean War. Photo created 1998 and provided by the National Archives.

---

[98] Oh, Arissa H. *To Save the Children of Korea: The Cold War Origins of International Adoption.* Stanford: Stanford University Press, 2015. Page 8.
[99] Sacerdote, Bruce. "How Large are the Effects from the Changes in Family Environment? A Study of Korean American Adoptees." *The Quarterly Journal of Economics* 122, no. 1 (2007). 119–157.

A Korean girl tiredly trudges her brother on her back in Haengju,
Korea during the Korean War. National Archives photo.

Holt International's and the American media's portrayal of children
orphaned by the Korean War as waifs tugged at the hearts of U.S. evan-
gelicals.[100] In total, American families adopted more than half of Korea's
orphans. The surge in adoption of Korean children continued for years
after the war. By 1977, Holt International had succeeded in bringing
approximately 35,000 Korean adoptees to the United States. Adoption of
Korean children continues today and those that were brought over illegally
or without proper paper work face several problems regarding citizenship
as well as difficulties with their new families. Today, Korean adoptees who
came years after the Korean War ended, face deportation as the Deferred
Action for Childhood Arrivals (DACA) immigration policy enacted by
the Obama administration, was rescinded under Trump's presidency on
September 5, 2017. Since then, many states have challenged the Trump
administrations order to rescind DACA. At the time of publication of this

---

[100] Kim, Eleana. "The Origins of Korean Adoption: Cold War Geopolitics and
Intimate Diplomacy." *U.S.-Korea Institute's Working Paper Series*, WP 09-09, October
2009.

textbook, the U.S. Citizenship and Immigration Services (USCIS) web site updated its information about the status of DACA with the following:

> USCIS is not accepting requests from individuals who have never before been granted deferred action under DACA. Due to federal court orders on Jan. 9, 2018 and Feb. 13, 2018 USCIS has resumed accepting requests to renew a grant of deferred action under DACA. The scope of the Feb. 13 preliminary injunction issued in the Eastern District of New York is the same as the Jan. 9 preliminary injunction issued in the Northern District of California. Unless otherwise provided in this guidance, the DACA policy will be operated on the terms in place before it was rescinded on Sept. 5, 2017, until further notice.[101]

DACA allows immigrants who were brought to the United States illegally as children, to request consideration of deferred removal action for a period of two years, subject to renewal. DACA applicants are eligible if they arrived before their 16th birthday and were at least 15 or under the age of 31 on June 15, 2012, living in the U.S. and continuously so since June 15, 2007, in school, a high school graduate, or have obtained a GED when applying, according to the policy. Applicants can also be an honorably discharged veteran of the U.S. Armed Forces or Coast Guard to be eligible. However, applicants who have been convicted of a felony, a significant misdemeanor, are deemed ineligible for the program, according to the Department of Homeland Security's web site.[102]

Many of the parents who adopted Korean children over the last several decades, didn't know they had to, or neglected to naturalize their children. In May 2018, 48,000 of the 1.326 million undocumented young adults

---

[101] "Deferred Action for Childhood Arrivals: Response to January 2018 Preliminary Injunction." U.S. Citizenship and Immigration Services. February 14, 2018 Update. https://www.uscis.gov/humanitarian/deferred-action-childhood-arrivals-response-january-2018-preliminary-injunction. Retrieved February 23, 2019.

[102] "DACA." Department of Homeland Security. https://www.dhs.gov/deferred-action-childhood-arrivals-daca. Retrieved February 23, 2019.

eligible for DACA were of Korean heritage; and 7,180 applied for and were approved for the program. (See Table 2)[103]

Table 2

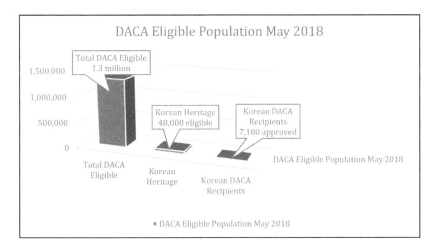

Korean War Brides and the Korean American Community

Many American "G.I."[104] troops coming home from the Korean War brought back Korean wives. These so-called "G.I. brides" played an instrumental role in the future of Korean immigration to the United States. During the Korean War, American soldiers married Korean women. When the war came to a cease-fire on July 27, 1953, the soldiers took their

---

[103] "Deferred Action for Childhood Arrivals (DACA) Data Tools." Migration Policy Institute. May 2018. https://www.migrationpolicy.org/programs/data-hub/deferred-action-childhood-arrivals-daca-profiles.

[104] O'Conner, Patricia T., and Stewart Kellerman. *Origins of the Specious: Myths and Misconceptions of the English Language*. New York: Random House, 2010.

The origin of the term "G.I." is not clear. A prominent theory suggests that "G.I." originated in the early twentieth century when the acronym "G.I." was marked on military trash cans and buckets. At the time, "G.I." stood for "galvanized iron," the metal the trash cans and buckets were made from. Later, during World War I, the term "G.I." broadened to include everything Army-related. Thus, the term "G.I." expanded and included the definition of "general issue" or "government issue." By the time of the Korean War, soldiers were already being referred to as G.I.s.

Korean-born wives back to the United States with them.[105] In fact, of the 14,027 Koreans who came to the U.S. between 1950 and 1964, 6,423 were Korean women who were married to American soldiers.[106]

The lives of the Korean war brides were similar with those of the picture brides who came to U.S. territories during the early 1900s, when Korean men worked as sugar plantation laborers in Hawaii. War brides faced language barriers, cultural differences, and were often abused by their husbands. They faced harsh realities, suffering abuse and mental health issues, and thus, many G.I. marriages ended in divorce. One of the biggest challenges Korean war brides faced was the psychological isolation they felt; their families were still in Korea. Some of the Korean war brides regretted leaving their families who were not allowed to follow them. However, U.S. immigration law changed in 1965, when Congress passed the Immigration and Nationality Act (or the Hart-Celler Act). The act abolished the quota system that had restricted immigration based on national origin, especially for those of Asian heritage, and called for reuniting immigrant families and bringing skilled labor to the U.S. The Korean war brides could now send for their parents and siblings. According to some scholars, 40 percent of Korean immigration to the United States in the 1960s and 1970s can be attributed to GI brides who sent for their families:

> Although frequently overlooked, some of the women in this group should be regarded as the principal founders of the Korean American community as we know it today. This is because many of the later immigrants were relatives whom the 'war brides' sponsored. These women deserve to be thanked for the safe settlement of their family members.[107]

The Korean American community slowly grew in number between the 1940s and 1960s with the arrival of students, diplomats, war brides and their families, and adoptees. The total Korean American population

---

[105] Yu, Dina. *Winds of Change: Korean Women in America*. Silver Spring, Maryland: The Women's Institute Press, 1995. Page 241.
[106] Ibid.
[107] Ibid.

by 1950 was 7,030. In 1960, the U.S. Census Bureau didn't collect specific data on Koreans; the prevailing thought was that there were not enough Koreans to count at the time, and therefore, they were not included in the data set.[108] Korean America remained small in comparison to the Chinese and Japanese American communities, but with the help of the Korean war brides, the Korean American community grew dramatically. By the 1970s, the Korean American population totaled almost 70,000, a figure that would continue to climb.[109]

Korean American Highlight
Col. Young Oak Kim

Young Oak Kim as a U.S. Army Lieutenant Colonel in 1965.

Born and raised in Los Angeles, California, Young Oak Kim was a Korean American war hero who served in World War II and the Korean War. Kim's parents, Soon Kwan Kim and Nora Ko migrated to the United

---

[108] "Korean-American Population 1910–2010." KoreanAmericanStory.org. November 23, 2011. http://koreanamericanstory.org/korean-american-population-1910-2010/.
[109] Min, Pyong Gap, and Chigon Kim. "Growth of the Korean Population and Changes in Their Settlement Patterns Over Time, 1990-2008." Queens, New York: Research Center for Korean Community, Queens College of CUNY. Research Report No. 2. March 16, 2010.

States in the early 1900s. Kim's father worked on a Hawaiian sugar plantation before moving to Los Angeles. Kim's father was also a dedicated Korean independence activist. Mr. and Mrs. Kim had six children, four boys and two girls. Young Oak was the eldest son. His sister, Willa, was the eldest of the children. She became a highly respected and famous costume designer, winning Tony Awards for her work on Broadway shows. Young Oak Kim went to Belmont High School in Los Angeles. He later attended Los Angeles City College, but after one year, he dropped out. He wasn't happy with the racial discrimination he saw, nor the fact that, despite his friends earning college degrees, they still ended up working at small businesses like grocery markets.[110]

When World War II broke out and the United States joined the Allied Forces in 1941, Kim wanted to join the Army. At first, he was denied entry due to anti-Asian policies. However, the draft was enacted, and all men, no matter their ethnicity, were included. Kim went to the United States Army's Officer Candidate School in Fort Benning, Georgia, where he graduated in January 1943 as a second lieutenant. Kim was assigned to the 100th Battalion. The unit was comprised of mostly Japanese Americans. During World War II, the United States questioned the loyalty of Japanese Americans. Executive Order 9066 was issued by President Franklin D. Roosevelt, calling for the interment of 120,000 Japanese Americans. The 100th Battalion was made up of family members of these interned Japanese Americans who were labeled as resident alien enemies.[111]

When Kim arrived in Hawaii to help lead the 100th, his commanding officer recommended a transfer when he realized Kim was Korean. Kim refused, saying they were all fighting for the same side and they were all Americans. Kim stayed with the unit and trained them for months before they were finally shipped to North Africa for their first tour of duty. The unit would earn numerous medals and honors. Young Oak, who was wounded in action, also earned recognitions including the Distinguished Service Cross, two Silver Stars, two Bronze Stars, three Purple Hearts, and two Legions of Merit. Kim would also earn the Military Valor Cross and

---

[110] Han, Woo Sung and Edward T. Chang. *Unsung Hero: The Story of Col. Young Oak Kim*. Riverside, California: Young Oak Kim Center, University of California Riverside Press, 2011.

[111] Ibid.

the Bronze Cross of Military Valor from Italy, and the Legion d'Honneur from France, for his actions during World War II.[112]

After the war, Young Oak was honorably discharged from the Army. He went back to Los Angeles, where he decided to try his hand at business. He opened what might have been the first coin laundry on 6th Street and Bixel in downtown Los Angeles.[113] The business flourished, but then, in June 1950, the Korean War broke out, and Kim decided to reenlist. He sold his business and volunteered. The U.S. Army had already taken measures to contact him at the time because they needed Korean-speaking soldiers. Kim, who was now a major, received orders to report to an Army base near San Francisco on September 25, 1950. He was assigned to the 31st Infantry of the 7th Infantry Division as chief intelligence officer and *de facto* operations officer by Col. William J. McCaffrey. The 31st Infantry won almost every battle it fought and pushed further north than anyone expected. By accident, the 555th Field Artillery Battalion once mistook Kim's battalion as the enemy and opened fire; Kim was seriously wounded. He was sent to Tokyo where he was treated by doctors from Johns Hopkins University who used then-experimental penicillin treatments. Two months after being wounded, Major Kim was back in Korea.

Col. McCaffrey decided to reassign Kim to command the 1st Battalion, 31st Infantry of the U.S. Army, and Kim became the first ethnic minority to command an Army battalion on the battlefield. He served in the Korean War with honor and earned the Korean Taegeuk Order of Military Merit for his bravery. During the Korean War, Kim's compassion and humanitarian side also displayed itself. His 1st Battalion became the only unit of the U.S. Army to adopt an orphanage during the Korean War. The unit supported the orphanage in Seoul, Korea, and donated food, toys, money, and their time to the children.

Young Oak Kim continued his military career after the Korean War and retired in 1972 as a colonel. He went back to Los Angeles, where he kept a promise he made to himself during World War II: "If I survive this war, I will devote my life to the betterment of the community I belong to."[114] He did exactly that. After dealing with health issues and complications from

---

[112] Ibid.

[113] Ibid.

[114] Ibid.

his battle wounds, Col. Kim found himself with the hope and the desire to help others. He became a public servant and was the founding father of the Korean Health Education and Information Research Center in Los Angeles. He also played a major role in the founding and funding of the Koreatown Youth and Community Center in Los Angeles. Col. Kim also helped found Los Angeles' Korean American Museum. In the 1980s, Col. Kim helped protect women and children as chairman of Every Woman's Shelter in Los Angeles.

Most notably, Col. Kim helped develop the Korean American Coalition, a major voice for the Korean American community today, with chapters all over the United States. Col. Kim was chairman of the Go for Broke Foundation, a World War II Japanese American veterans' association. The foundation became the Go for Broke National Education Center, and in 1999, Col. Kim helped raise funds for the Go for Broke Monument in downtown Los Angeles.

Col. Kim's life and military career have been honored by various organizations, countries, and people. While he has received the equivalent of the Medal of Honor from France, Italy, and Korea, he has not received it from his birth country, the United States.

CHAPTER 5

KOREAN AMERICAN COMMUNITY POST-1965 IMMIGRATION ACT

Known as "new urban immigrants," post-1965 Korean immigrants found themselves in an America that had just experienced the civil rights movement and desegregation. By the 1970s, Korean Americans were largely located in Los Angeles County, owning and operating stores in inner cities that included South Central Los Angeles. Other Korean Americans lived and worked in places like Chicago, Illinois; Dallas, Texas; Flushing, Queens, New York; and Baltimore, Maryland.

The strong concentration of Koreans in Los Angeles County can be explained by several factors. Prior to the 1965 Immigration Act, Koreans had already carved out a Koreatown in Los Angeles' Bunker Hill neighborhood, near the University of Southern California campus. Thus, when the post-1965 Korean immigrants arrived, they made their way to Los Angeles where they felt welcomed and had access to *ethclass* resources.[115] The immigrants also came to the U.S. unaware of the race relations, class lines, and intergroup conflicts that plagued the American landscape.

Instead, Korean immigrants relied upon their ethnic community for support, funding, and guidance in their new American lives; they remained sheltered from the larger socioeconomic issues of their host country. Many Korean immigrants found their "American Dream" by opening small businesses like grocery markets, gas stations, liquor stores,

---

[115] *Ethclass* resources refers to combination of ethnic and class-based resources Korean immigrants brought with them from Korea.

and wig shops in inner-city communities like South Central Los Angeles, a predominantly African American area.

African Americans first began moving to South Central Los Angeles and other inner-city communities after World War II. Known as "Defense Migration," the expansion of industrial plants and chronic labor shortages during the war opened defense job opportunities to minorities. The plethora of jobs attracted a new wave of African Americans to California, who found work in ship building, aircraft manufacturing, and the rubber industry.[116] By the 1940s and 1950s, the cities of Compton and Watts in Los Angeles County became predominantly black. By 1940, the demographics of South Central Los Angeles shifted dramatically; the area was 70 percent African American.[117] At the same time, the white residents of those communities left the area for the suburbs in what was known as "White Flight." The white population feared that the influx of the African American community would cause the value of their homes to drop significantly, so they sold their properties and left, moving to places like Irvine in Orange County. Thus, when Koreans began opening shops in these inner-city communities, they were moving into ironically recently desegregated areas that were now predominantly African American.

The inner-city communities would further change as deindustrialization and globalization in the 1970s and 1980s changed the American economic structure. Companies sent production offshore, and imports like Japanese automobiles pushed the U.S. economy further into service-based industries and away from manufacturing.[118]

Korean Americans were not welcomed with open arms by the African American community not just in South Central Los Angeles, but also in New York and other states throughout the country. The Koreans that came to the U.S. in the late 1960s and 1970s were mostly educated and arrived with some money. However, their skills were not transferable in the U.S., and they experienced the same corporate discrimination and racism as

---

[116] Collins, Keith. *Black Los Angeles: The Maturing of the Ghetto, 1940-1950*. Saratoga, California: Century Twenty-One Publishing, 1980. Page 9.

[117] De Graaf, Lawrence B. "Negro Migration to Los Angeles, 1930-1950." PhD diss, University of California at Los Angeles, 1962.

[118] Chang, Edward T., and Jeanette Diaz-Veizades. *Ethnic Peace in the American City*. New York: New York University Press, 1999. Page 61.

other minorities. Unable to find jobs, these new immigrants found themselves buying businesses from Jewish Americans. Unbeknownst to the new Korean immigrants, the Jewish American business owners were leaving the inner cities because of the race riots—including the 1965 Watts Riots in Los Angeles County—violence, and crime. The cultural and economic differences, not to mention the language barriers, between Korean immigrants and African American inner-city residents would set the foundation of a more-than-twenty-year misunderstanding between the two communities. As stated by Chang and Diaz-Veizades (1999), for African Americans, "Korean stores represented the economic disenfranchisement at the hands of the white oppressors and their Asian surrogates."[119]

Korean American journalist K.W. (Kyung Won) Lee, the godfather of Asian American journalism, covered desegregation and discrimination in the Jim Crow South during the 1950s. However, his work was not widely read by Korean Americans. Lee was the first Asian American immigrant to be hired by a mainstream American newspaper. He reported for the *Kingsport Times and News* in Tennessee and the *Charleston Gazette* in West Virginia. Lee's investigate coverage of the civil rights movement would earn recognition from the California Newspaper Publishers Association and the John Anson Ford Award from the Human Relations Commission of Los Angeles County. His vast experience covering racism would help give voice to the Korean American community.

Notably, Lee wrote a series of investigative articles for the *Sacramento Union* on the case of the wrongfully convicted Chol Soo Lee in the 1970s. Chol Soo Lee was the victim of racial profiling and was imprisoned for a murder he didn't commit in San Francisco's Chinatown. The articles K.W. Lee wrote about his case gained national and international attention. The Korean American and the Asian American communities mobilized and demanded a retrial of Chol Soo Lee's case. The Free Chol Soo Lee Defense Committee became the first pan-Asian American justice movement. K.W. Lee wrote more than 100 articles about Chol Soo Lee. Ultimately, the case was retried, and the conviction was overturned.

In the 1970s and 1980s, K.W. Lee believed that the Korean American community lacked political voice and community organization. In 1979, he founded the *Koreatown Weekly*; it was the first national English-language,

---

[119] Ibid.

Korean American news publication. The newspaper embodied efforts to bridge cultural gaps between the African American and Korean American communities through objective reporting.

Koreatown in Los Angeles

Today, the largest Korean American community is in California, with more than 500,000 Korean Americans living in the state. Of that number, more than 330,000 Koreans lived in Los Angeles County in 2015.[120]

Koreatown in Los Angeles is the heart and capital of Korean America. The transnational enclave developed during the early 1970s. Prior to that, during the 1930s and 1940s, Koreans were mainly living in downtown Los Angeles' Bunker Hill section; it was one of the few locations that allowed non-white residents at the time. The Korean community grew and shifted toward Jefferson Boulevard and the current University of Southern California campus.[121] This area became a hub for Korean immigrants, who were able to access political and religious support, as well as financial and medical assistance from those who spoke their language.

The Bunker Hill Korean community thrived, and when the next wave of Korean immigrants came to the United States, after the passage of the 1965 Immigration Act, the small community became saturated. Meanwhile, Los Angeles' Wilshire District began to change. In 1957, the city revised its building height restrictions and allowed for high-rise commercial buildings to spring up. Many of the residents moved west to suburbia, allowing for denser development to take place. Lower rents and commercial real estate opportunities drew the Korean community away from the Bunker Hill area to Olympic Boulevard in Los Angeles.

---

[120] Pew Research Center analysis of 2013-2015 American Community Survey (IPUMS). Based on mixed-race and mixed-group populations, regardless of Hispanic origin. See methodology for more details.
[121] "L.A.'s K-Town: Culture and Community." Los Angeles: Los Angeles Conservancy. November 3-5, 2017. www.laconservancy.org/ktown.

Figueroa Street, looking north towards 1ˢᵗ Street, with house
occupied by the Korean National Association and Ahn Chang
Ho in sight in Los Angeles' Bunker Hill area.
Image courtesy of the Korean American Digital Archive, USC.

The opening of the Olympic Market in 1969 and later, various Korean restaurants in the 1970s along Olympic Boulevard, heralded the beginning of L.A.'s Koreatown as we know it today. Korean Americans opened stores, restaurants, and other shops in the Wilshire District's strip malls and along Olympic Boulevard, Western Avenue, and Vermont Avenue.[122] By 1976, more than 70,000 Koreans resided in the area of Olympic Boulevard and 8ᵗʰ Street between Crenshaw Boulevard and Hoover Street.[123] The area was also home to more than 1,000 Korean businesses.[124]

In the aftermath of the L.A. Riots in 1992, many white-owned businesses and corporations along Wilshire Boulevard relocated to the west side of the city, which provided opportunities to the Korean businesses.

---

[122] Ibid.

[123] "Los Angeles Citywide Historic Context Statement: Korean Amerians in Los Angeles, 1905-1980." SurveyLA, City of Los Angeles Office of Historic Resources. National Register of Historic Places Multiple Property Documentation Form: Korean Americans. April 2018.

[124] Ibid.

Korean-owned shops continued to dominate the Wilshire District, moving along 6th Street and northward. Today, Koreatown's demographics include primarily Hispanic residents, though Korean-owned businesses still make up most of the storefronts.

Koreatown in Manhattan, New York

The Korean American population in New York was about 211,000 in 2015, while the total population of the state was estimated at about 19.8 million. New York is home to the second largest Korean population in the United States. (Los Angeles is number one).[125]

In Manhattan, New York, a Koreatown developed in the late 1970s and early 1980s. Similar to what had happened in Los Angeles, low rents in New York's Garment District and in Midtown, near the Empire State Building, coupled with high pedestrian traffic, and the promise of economic success, attracted Korean immigrants. Once again, Korean immigrants relied on *ethclass* resources, their own financial savings, and community support to open businesses in Manhattan. While a market started Los Angeles' Koreatown, Manhattan's Koreatown began with the establishment of Koryo Books around 1978. Soon after the bookstore's opening, other Korean-themed restaurants, markets, and shops opened their doors, and New York's Koreatown was inadvertently established.[126]

The development of New York's Koreatown involved grocers, restaurants, shops, and other businesses owned and operated by Korean immigrants. In fact, Korean-owned merchants would later make headlines as their conflict and culture clash with inner-city African American residents escalated. As the area continued to grow and flourish along 32nd Street, the gathering of Korean businesses in District 5 in Manhattan became

---

[125] "Top 10 U.S. metropolitan areas by Korean population, 2015." Pew Research Center analysis of 2013-2015 American Community Survey (IPUMS). September 7, 2015. http://www.pewsocialtrends.org/chart/top-10-u-s-metropolitan-areas-by-korean-population/.

[126] Berger, Joseph, and Chris Caruso. "The People of New York: The History of Koreatown." New York: Macaulay Honors College at City College, Seminar 2, 2010. https://macaulay.cuny.edu/eportfolios/berger2010/a-taste-of-the-world/the-history-of-koreatown/.

known as Korea Way in 1995.[127] Today, Koreatown, New York, is located on West 32nd Street (Korea Way) between Madison Avenue and the intersection of Sixth Avenue and Broadway. New York's Koreatown mirrors Los Angeles' with respect to its reputation as an ethnic enclave; a hub for all things Korean.

A picture of the Korea Way and 32nd street signs in New York in 2013.

Korean American Identity: 1960s-1980s

When Koreans first came to the United States in the early 1900s, they viewed themselves as Korean nationals. During the Japanese occupation of Korea from 1910 to 1945, Koreans all over the world saw themselves as patriots fighting for the freedom of their homeland. In the United States, Koreans worked fervently toward the independence movement; they viewed themselves as refugees, living in political asylum, while they fought for their motherland.

However, after the end of World War II and the subsequent freedom of Korea, Koreans in the United States found themselves focused on a new

---

[127] Ibid.

life, despite the racism and discrimination prohibiting them, along with other Asians, from integrating into mainstream American society. Instead, Koreans in the United States continued to live in their ethnic enclaves without representation, communication, or much social interaction with the surrounding communities.

By the 1970s, the Korean American community began to grow. The influx of the new urban immigrants didn't bring much change to the identity of the existing Korean American community. Instead, these new Korean immigrants viewed themselves as Koreans living in America, not as Korean Americans. Although, some second-generation Korean Americans participated in civil rights movements including anti-war, women's and Asian American movements, and politics, most of the Korean community did not. Alfred Song was one of those few Korean Americans who participated in politics, he was elected to the city council of Monterrey Park in April 1960, making him the first person of Korean ancestry to obtain such a position. In 1962, Dosan Ahn Chang Ho's eldest son, Philip Ahn was named honorary mayor of Panorama City, having starred in over two hundred films and television productions. In that same year, Song was elected to the California State Assembly; he was the first Asian-American to join the legislature.

While several Korean Americans did join in the 1968 San Francisco State College Strike and the fight to free Chol Soo Lee in the 1970s, many remained insular and silent. The 1960s and 1970s, therefore, was a quiet period for Korean Americans' public voice and identity. Instead, Korean Americans continued to be occupied with homeland politics, the reunification of North and South Korea, and the post-Korean War conditions of their motherland during this time. For example, in March 1963, six Koreans, including Choi Kyong-nok, a retired general in the Korean army; protested in front of the White House against the Korean military government.

During the 1970s and early 1980s, the Korean American community continued its focus on homeland politics. As the population of Korean Americans grew, so did services for them; in 1971 Korean Air opened a Los Angeles branch office and operated its first freight flight to Los Angeles. In 1972, several organizations were established for the Korean American community including: the Korean American Youth Foundation; the

Medical Health Service Center for Koreans in Los Angeles; and the Korean American Cultural Association. Throughout the 1970s, Korean American community organizations continued to be established and included business-oriented associations like the Korean Restaurants Association of Southern California and the Korean Food Products Manufacturers' Association of Southern California.

During the 1970s, the Korean martial art, taekwondo, also became hugely popular in the United States. Born in Asan Korea in 1932, Jhoon Goo Rhee, who is considered the father of American taekwondo, began teaching the martial art in Texas in 1956. Taekwondo, which means the way of the foot and fist, gained recognition in the United States. Rhee organized the Congressional Taekwondo Club in 1965 and trained several politicians including former Vice President Joe Biden.[128] By the 1970s, Rhee became a local household name in Washington after he began broadcasting television commercials.[129] While Rhee was not the first person to teach taekwondo, he popularized the martial art through his network of schools, commercials, and by creating modern safety equipment for the sport. Today, taekwondo is a widely recognized sport practiced in the United States and all over the world.[130]

By the 1980s, the Korean American community had established roots all over the United States, yet they remained outside of mainstream American politics. Even though things like taekwondo helped to improve Korean American visibility, it wasn't enough to stave off the misunderstandings, the cultural gaps, and the differences that would later plague them.

---

[128] Smith, Harrison. Jhoon Rhee, who helped popularize taekwondo in the United States, dies at 86." *Washington Post*. May 1, 2018. Obituaries. https://www.washingtonpost.com/local/obituaries/jhoon-rhee-who-helped-popularize-taekwondo-in-the-united-states-dies-at-86/2018/05/01/db60f3da-4d45-11e8-af46-b1d-6dc0d9bfe_story.html?utm_term=.e51d240d8b03. Accessed March 11, 2019.

[129] Ibid.

[130] Ibid.

Korean Americans and the Model Minority

The new urban Korean immigrants and Asian Americans of the 1970s and 1980s fell into the trap of the model minority. In 1966, an article published by *New York Times Magazine* titled, "Success Story, Japanese American Style," gave birth to the myth of the model minority. The article described the seeming success of Japanese Americans, despite being interned in 1942 by the U.S. government during World War II. The article pointed out that Japanese Americans were adjusting back into society, working hard, and not complaining; they were the model minority.

The term soon applied to all Asian Americans, including the new urban Korean immigrant, who came to the U.S. to work hard, pull himself up by the bootstraps, and live the American Dream. The flawed term pitted minorities against each other, and Korean Americans, who largely owned and operated businesses in predominantly African American neighborhoods, were caught in the middle. Korean Americans were also the largest self-employed group within the Asian American community at the time and continued to be so in 2000; 19.1 percent of the Korean American population was self-employed, with the next Asian group self-employed at 13.6 percent in that year, according to the U.S. Census Bureau. Korean Americans also worked long hours and relied on family for help running their businesses. Often, Korean parents utilized their children as laborers.

In the 1970s and 1980s, Korean immigrants struggled to assimilate into American society. Many attended Korean churches, read Korean-language newspapers, and were caught up in homeland politics. The Korean Consulate of Los Angeles, along with the Korean Central Intelligence Agency, the Korean Association, and ethnic media formed an alliance to control Korean American political views.

By the 1980s, Korean immigrants also lived outside of the inner-city communities their businesses were part of, typically in suburban locations. For example, in California, many Korean immigrants lived in Torrance, San Fernando Valley, Diamond Bar, San Francisco, Fullerton, Cerritos, and Irvine. The geographic divide between an inner city's business community and its residents grew to drive a wedge between Korean American business owners and their African American clientele.

Korean American Highlight
Kyung Won "K.W." Lee

Kyung Won Lee speaks to a crowd during a panel discussion at the Asian American Journalism Association convention in Los Angeles on August 7, 2007. Photo courtesy of Hyungwon Kang.

Kyung Won "K.W." Lee was born in Kaesong, North Korea, in 1928. He attended Korea University in Seoul, South Korea. During World War II Lee was recruited by the Japanese Army as an expendable combat air cadet. He was barely 16 years old. The bombing of Hiroshima and Nagasaki stopped the war, and Lee escaped with his life. In 1950, he immigrated to the United States on a student visa and became a journalism major at West Virginia University. In 1955, he obtained a master's degree from the University of Illinois and became the first Asian immigrant to be hired by a mainstream American newspaper. Lee reported for the *Kingsport Times and News* in Tennessee. He also reported for the *Charleston Gazette* in West Virginia.

In the 1970s, Lee reported for the *Sacramento Union*. While working for the California-based paper, Lee wrote a series of investigative stories on Chol Soo Lee, a Korean immigrant wrongly convicted for a murder he didn't commit. Ultimately, Chol Soo Lee was freed. *True Believer*, a Hollywood film based on the Chol Soo Lee case, premiered in 1989 and neglected to give credit to K.W. Lee for his work, instead showcasing Lee's lawyer, played by white American actor James Woods.

In 1979, K.W. Lee saw the need for a voice in the Korean American community. He founded the *Koreatown Weekly*, which was the first national English-language Korean American newspaper. After three years, the paper folded in 1982. In 1987, Lee and several other Korean American reporters founded the Korean American Journalists Association. Then, in 1990, Lee founded the *Korea Times English Edition* in Los Angeles in order to cover the tension between the Korean and African American communities. During the 1992 L.A. Riots, Lee was hospitalized due to a Hepatitis B infection; he received a liver transplant. Despite his illness, Lee made sure his reporters covered the watershed event. However, the *Korea Times English Edition* folded later that year.

After his second paper folded, K.W. Lee continued to serve the Korean American community through journalism. Lee received numerous awards including the John Anson Ford Award by the Human Relations Commission of Los Angele and the Free Spirit Award from the Freedom Forum in 1994. (He was the first Asian American to receive the Free Spirit Award). In 1997, he was inducted into the Newseum's Journalism History Gallery.

Today, K.W. Lee speaks at conferences, universities, and other special events about Korean American history. In 2003, the K.W. Lee Center for Leadership was founded in Los Angeles and provides leadership opportunities, training, and education for young adults and children. In 2016, he published his series of articles in Korean entitled *Lonesome Journey: The Korean American Century* in Korea. Lee is now in semi-retirement, but his passion for raising the voice of the Korean American community holds strong.[131]

Korean American Highlight
Jacqueline Eurn Hai Young

Born on May 20, 1934, in Honolulu, Hawaii, Jacqueline E. Young was the first Korean American woman to serve as a legislator when she was elected to the Hawaii State House of Representatives in 1990. Her

---

[131] The information in the K.W. Lee highlight was pulled from several interviews of Lee over the course of several years. The interviews are archived and transcribed and housed at the YOK Center, UC Riverside.

grandparents were among the first pioneering Korean immigrants to land in Hawaii during the early 1900s. Her grandfather was a prolific Korean independence activist.

Jacqueline Young earned a Ph.D. in communication and women's studies from the Union Institute of Ohio in 1989. In 1992, she was re-elected to the Hawaii State House of Representatives and became the first female vice speaker of the House. Young co-founded the Asian-Pacific Island National Caucus of Legislators. Known as a groundbreaking feminist, Young advocated for the equality of education for girls in public schools. She also helped found a domestic-violence shelter, Hale Ola, in Windward Oahu. Young retired from public office in 1994 and worked with the governor of Hawaii as director of the Office of Affirmative Action. She later founded J. Young Productions and produced televisions shows with focus on Hawaii. She died in February 2019.[132]

---

[132] Dayton, Kevin. "Former Hawaii lawmaker Jackie Young dies at 84." *Star Advertiser*. Honolulu, Hawaii. February 13, 2019. https://www.staradvertiser.com/2019/02/13/hawaii-news/former-hawaii-lawmaker-jackie-young-dies/. Accessed March 11, 2019.

CHAPTER 6

BLACK-KOREAN RACE
RELATIONS IN THE 1980S
AND THE 1992 LA RIOTS

In the 1960s and 1970s, the Korean community in America faded into the background. Politically and socially, Korean Americans were underrepresented during this time. Despite their political marginalization and underrepresentation, the Korean American population increased dramatically during this period, rising from about 70,000 in 1970 to 354,000 by 1980.[133]

During this time, Korean Americans were viewed as the "middleman minority"; they occupied the space between the "haves" and the "havenots." In other words, Korean Americans became the buffer between the affluent white and often poorer black and Latino communities. The African American community believed that Korean Americans were "ripping them off" by charging high prices. They also believed that Korean Americans were purposefully disrespectful by not greeting them or looking them in the eye. Meanwhile, Korean business owners viewed their black clientele with suspicion. Koreans who had failed to assimilate into American culture continued to treat their customers the way they did in

---

[133] Min, Pyong Gap, and Chigon Kim. "Growth of the Korean Population and Changes in Their Settlement Patterns Over Time, 1990-2008." Queens, New York: Research Center for Korean Community, Queens College of CUNY. Research Report No. 2. March 16, 2010.

Korea, where they were taught not to look customers in the eyes or count out change because it was considered rude. The two communities clearly didn't understand each other.

In the 1970s and 1980s, the Korean and African American communities would make headlines for the so-called "black-Korean conflict." Shootings of Korean American storeowners and African American customers, as well as numerous boycotts of Korean-owned shops all over the United States, would grab media attention in print and on television. However, the Korean American community had very little to no voice or representation in American politics and society; their identity was still tied to their nationalistic roots and they viewed themselves as Koreans in America, not Korean Americans. Thus, their media portrayal was nearly one sided as there were few organizations or leaders in the Korean American community who could speak for them.

Throughout the 1980s, the violence and conflict between the Korean and African American communities increased dramatically. Dozens of boycotts of Korean-owned stores—including boycotts of the Red Apple Market in Brooklyn, New York, and others in Los Angeles—demonstrated the deep divide between the two minorities.[134]

Meanwhile, the crack cocaine epidemic would change the African American community forever. Two dominant black gangs, the Bloods and the Crips, would fight for territory as they battled for the rights to sell this cheap, new drug. Crack hit the streets hard, and inner-city communities were affected immensely. The drug destroyed families and created more crime and gang violence in these neighborhoods. Due to President Reagan's War on Drugs, an attempt to crack down on drug use and violence in America's inner cities, by 1989, one in four African American men aged 20 to 29 was incarcerated, on probation, or on parole.[135] At the same time, the inner cities also experienced neglect in terms of education and investment. African Americans also suffered from police brutality.

---

[134] Min, Pyong Gap. *Caught in the Middle: Korean Merchants in America's Multiethnic Cities.* University of California Press. Berkley and Los Angeles, California. 1996. Pages 73-75.

[135] Turner, Deonna S. "Crack epidemic." *Encyclopaedia Britannica.* Last Updated: 4 Sept. 2017. www.britannica.com/topic/crack-epidemic.

These conditions, coupled with the black-Korean conflict, would stir the pot of unrest.

Amidst the violence and miscommunication, one organization formed to create dialogue between the Korean and African American communities. Founded in 1986, the Los Angeles Black-Korean Alliance (BKA) was created by the Los Angeles County Human Relations Commission. The group attempted to bridge cultural differences between the two minorities and help alleviate misunderstandings, but the black-Korean conflict continued. No end was in sight.

Despite the black-Korean conflict and racial discrimination, the Korean American community continued to grow and flourish in the 1980s. Korean Americans opened companies in the industrial and service sectors; a new wave of immigrants moved to Los Angeles to succeed as business owners; while still others became successful lawyers and doctors serving not just Los Angeles' Koreatown, but other communities throughout the United States as well. One Korean American, Dr. Myung Ki "Mike" Hong, founded DuraCoat Products Inc. in 1985, which became a major piping paints developer and manufacturer. However, as the Korean American community grew, with the population hitting 798,000 by 1990,[136] it continued to lack representation and voice in mainstream American politics and media. By 1991, only one Korean American had served as mayor of a California city: Jay Kim. He was mayor of Diamond Bar.

The Beating of Rodney King and the Shooting of Latasha Harlins

On March 3, 1991, motorist Rodney King was pulled over after leading police on a high-speed pursuit. King exited his vehicle and was surrounded by police officers. At the same time, George Holliday, a man who lived in a nearby apartment complex, pulled out his video camera and began recording. Four police officers pulled out their batons and Taser guns and beat King. Even in an age without smartphones, the video would go viral; news stations across the country broadcast it repeatedly. The footage would incite the anger of the African American community,

---

[136] "Korean-American Population 1910–2010." KoreanAmericanStory.org. November 23, 2011. http://koreanamericanstory.org/korean-american-population-1910-2010/.

who demanded justice for King. The four officers involved in the beating would later go to trial. The incident would later directly affect the Korean American community.

Thirteen days later, Korean shop owner Soon Ja Du shot and killed 15-year-old Latasha Harlins. The incident was also caught on tape. The footage shows Harlins and Du in a heated argument. Du could be seen accusing Harlins of shoplifting a bottle of juice, which Harlins denied. The two engaged in a scuffle, in which Du snatched Harlins' backpack and Harlins punched Du in the face. Later, Harlins left the bottle of juice on the counter and walked away.[137] That's when Du pulled out a gun and shot Harlins in the back of the head. Television media would show the footage repeatedly. Just as the beating of Rodney King would worsen already sour relations between black and white communities, the shooting of Latasha Harlins would further deepen the mistrust and conflict between the Korean and African American communities. The two incidents—the Rodney King beating and the shooting of Latasha Harlins—would fuel the racial tension and anger that led to the 1992 L.A. Riots.

The Los Angeles Riots: *Sa-i-gu*

On April 29, 1992, the Los Angeles Riots broke out after the four police officers in the Rodney King beating case received not-guilty verdicts. The verdicts were another racial and discriminatory blow to the African American community. The highly covered trial was held at the Simi Valley Courthouse in Ventura County, after it was moved from Los Angeles County; it was ruled that political and community divisiveness would not allow a jury from the area to be impartial in their judgement.[138] After the verdicts were read, many African American and Latino residents of inner-city communities in Los Angeles took to the streets, protesting the

---

[137] Ford, Andrea. "Videotape Shows Teen Being Shot After Figt: Killing: Trial opens for Korean grocer who is Accused in the slaying of a 15-year-old black girl at a South-Central store." *The Los Angeles Times*. October 1, 1991. http://articles.latimes. com/1991-10-01/local/me-3692_1_black-girl. Retrieved February 23, 2019.

[138] Serrano, Richard A. "King Case Shifts to Courtroom in Simi Valley." *The Los Angeles Times*. February 4, 1992. http://articles.latimes.com/1992-02-04/news/mn-1206_1_simi-valley. Retrieved February 23, 2019.

verdicts, racism, and discrimination. Unfortunately, violence began soon after on the corner of Normandie and Florence Avenues. The first store to be looted and destroyed was Tom's Liquor.

Armed volunteers guard California market from the roof in Koreatown, Los Angeles, California on May 1, 1992, on the third day of the 1992 L.A. Riots. Photo courtesy of Hyungwon Kan/*Los Angeles Times.*

Korean American business owners were caught in the crossfire of violence. During the civil unrest, many Korean business owners found themselves on their own, as the Los Angeles Police Department abandoned Koreatown. Rioters and looters ransacked and destroyed businesses. Left to fend for themselves, Korean Americans mounted their own defense.[139] Armed with guns and weapons, many Korean American business owners went to their stores to protect them. The owner of the first Hannam Market in Koreatown went to his shop and climbed up the roof with a group of his friends and his security guard. The group exchanged gunfire with rioters and would-be looters. The security guard was shot and killed.

---

[139] Lah, Kyung. "The LA riots were a rude awakening for Korea-Americans." CNN. April 29, 2017. https://www.cnn.com/2017/04/28/us/la-riots-korean-americans/index.html.

The owner continued his vigil at the market during the six days of civil unrest.[140]

Korean Americans, whose place in American society was still silent and ignored, turned to their ethnic radio and newspaper outlets for information and instructions. Radio Korea became the lifeline for many Korean American business owners at this time, while mainstream American media depicted Korean Americans as gun-toting vigilantes. Angela Oh, a prominent Korean American attorney, went on the news show *Night Line* to talk about the Korean American community.[141] She gave voice to the voiceless Korean immigrant victims of the L.A. Riots, which had wreaked havoc on Koreatown and neighboring communities including but not limited to Compton, Pasadena, Pomona, Inglewood, and others. At 8:45 p.m. on April 29, 1992, Los Angeles Mayor Tom Bradley declared a state of emergency and requested the aid of the National Guard. Governor Pete Wilson complied and also requested 2,000 National Guard troops.[142]

On April 30, 1992, a sunset-to-sunrise curfew was declared for Los Angeles County. Later in the day the National Guard was deployed. An additional 4,000 National Guard troops were requested by both the governor and the mayor. Meanwhile, Korean Americans engaged in gun battles with rioters and looters. Many Korean-owned shops were burned down and damaged, while black and Latino storeowners put "Latino Owned" or "Black Owned" signs in their windows to keep from being targeted.[143]

---

[140] Yi, Eugene. "SAIGU: An Oral History." *KoreAm Journal.* April 2012: 28-41. Print.

[141] Staff. "Out of Chaos, a New Voice: Angela Oh is emerging as a spokeswoman for Korean-Americans. 'I feel very strongly that people are capable of coming together.'" *The Los Angeles Times.* July 20, 1992. http://articles.latimes.com/1992-07-20/news/vw-4069_1_korean-american-community. Retrieved February 23, 2019.

[142] Park, Carol. *Memoir of a Cashier: Korean Americans, Racism, and Riots.* Riverside, California: YOK Center for Korean American Studies, University of California Riverside, 2017.

[143] Ibid.

A corner shopping center is fully engulfed in flames as it is left
burning out of control in Koreatown, Los Angeles, California
on May 1, 1992, the third day of the 1992 L.A. Riots.
Photo courtesy of Hyungwon Kang/*Los Angeles Times*.

On May 1, 1992, more than 1,000 Korean Americans and other individuals staged a peace rally at Western Avenue and Wilshire Boulevard
in Los Angeles. On that same day, Rodney King made his famous plea for
calm to the public asking, "Can we all get along?" Another 4,000 National
Guard troops were deployed.[144]

On May 2, 1992, approximately 30,000 people gathered in Koreatown
and marched for racial healing and peace. On May 3, 1992, the Reverend
Jesse Jackson arrived in Koreatown. He met with Korean and African
American leaders and urged for peace between the two communities.
Meanwhile, National Guard troops quelled the violence in various cities,
and peace began to take shape. By May 4, 1992, the riots were officially
over, and businesses, schools, and public transit resumed full operations.[145]

In total, the riots lasted for six days and more than 50 people lost their
lives, including one Korean American man, Eddie Lee. Korean Americans
suffered 40 percent, or $400 million of the $1 billion in damages and a total of 2,280 Korean American-owned stores were either destroyed, looted,
or suffered loss. The violence disillusioned the Korean American community, who call the event *Sa-i-gu*, or "four-two-nine," alluding to April 29,

---

[144] Ibid.
[145] Ibid.

the day the riots began. Many Korean Americans lost their livelihoods to the riots and were unable to recover. Liquor store owners were denied permits to rebuild. Other Korean Americans had no money to reopen their shops. The violence spread to other communities including San Francisco, Boston, Seattle, and even in Madison, Wisc.

The 1992 Los Angeles Riots awakened a sense of political activism in the Korean American community, whose struggle to rebuild was marked with racism and discrimination by the local government. The birth or rebirth of the Korean American identity occurred when the L.A. Riots ended. Korean American community leaders began to speak up, engage in local politics, and give back to the communities their businesses were part of.[146]

Although the Black Korean Alliance disbanded later that year, in December 1992, the relationship between the two communities would improve after the L.A. Riots for various reasons. The Korean and African American communities began to recognize that they needed one another. After the riots, many inner-city residents walked miles for their groceries because local Korean-owned markets were destroyed. Many Korean Americans also realized they needed to talk to their customers and bridge the cultural gaps. Although many Korean Americans moved away from Los Angeles to places like Orange County and the Inland Empire, those that remained worked to "get along" with their African American customers. In addition, many black residents moved to Rialto and other cities in the Inland Empire, as well as out of state. This demographic shift in Los Angeles helped calm animosity. By 2017, the majority of the population of Koreatown and in inner cities like Compton and Watts had shifted, becoming predominantly Hispanic. The demographics of business ownership also changed from Korean American to other Southeast Asian Americans,

---

[146] Constante, Agnes. "25 Years After LA Riots, Koreatown Finds Strength in 'Saigu' Legacy." *NBC News Asian America*. April 25, 2017. https://www.nbcnews.com/news/asian-america/25-years-after-la-riots-koreatown-finds-strength-saigu-legacy-n749081.

Arab Americans, and Egyptians. Today, the black-Korean conflict is not a major issue, but it still exists.[147]

As a result of *Sa-i-gu*, the Korean American community learned to give back to their greater local community; get involved in local and national politics; bridge cultural gaps through dialogue and understanding; and to build coalitions and organizations to help raise the voice of Korean Americans and find their identity in the public sphere.

After 1992, the Korean American community was no longer silent. Throughout the 1990s, the Korean American community became more visible. In Oregon, Republican John Lim was elected to the 11th District of the Oregon State Senate in November 1992. Lim served as majority leader in 1995 and was re-elected in 1996. Lim was then elected as state representative of District 50 in Oregon and was re-elected to that same position in 2006. Also, in 1992, Jay Kim, the mayor of Diamond Bar, California, was elected to the U.S. House of Representatives as a Republican. He was the first Korean American elected to the United States Congress. [148]

---

[147] Park, Carol. *Memoir of a Cashier: Korean Americans, Racism, and Riots.* Riverside, California: YOK Center for Korean American Studies, University of California Riverside, 2017.
[148] "Kim, Jay C." History, Art & Archives: United States House of Representatives. https://history.house.gov/People/Detail/16304.

Korean American Highlight
Angela Oh

Angela Oh giving opening remarks at the Hope Out of Crisis
event on April 28, 2012 in Koreatown, Los Angeles.

Born on September 8, 1955, Angela Oh is an attorney, a well-known teacher, and a public speaker. She received a Bachelor of Arts degree in 1977 from the University of California, Los Angeles, and graduated from the University of California, Davis School of Law in 1986. During the 1992 Los Angeles Riots, Oh served as a spokeswoman for the Korean American community, appearing on several television shows and was quoted in various newspapers.[149] She was appointed to President Bill Clinton's One America Initiative in the 21st Century: The President's Initiative on Race

---

[149] Yoshihara, Nancy. "Angela Oh: Adding an Asian American Voice to the Race Debate." *Los Angeles Times.* 13 July 1997. http://articles.latimes.com/1997/jul/13/opinion/op-12242.

advisory board in 1998. The board was tasked with helping engage the American people in a dialogue on race relations.

After the riots, Oh served as special counsel to the Assembly Special Committee on the Los Angeles Crisis. She also served as president of the Korean American Bar Association of Southern California. A prolific speaker, Oh has authored a collection of essays, *Open: One Woman's Journey*, which was published by the UCLA Asian American Studies Press in January 2002. Today, Oh is an ordained Zen Buddhist priest and continues her work as a Korean American community activist.

Korean American Highlight
Dr. Myung Ki Hong

Dr. Myung Ki Hong claps during a celebration in Koreatown, Los Angeles in 2015.

Born in Korea on June 20, 1934, Dr. Myung Ki "Mike" Hong emigrated to the United States in 1954. He graduated from the University of California, Los Angeles, in 1959 with a degree in chemistry. He became an expert chemist in resin and coatings. Dr. Hong later founded DuraCoat Products Inc. in Riverside, California. The company is well known for its high-performance industrial coatings. In 2016, DuraCoat became part of Axalta Coating Systems, a coatings supplier headquartered in Philadelphia.

Dr. Hong is more than a chemist and businessman. He is deeply involved in philanthropic, civic, and charitable causes, including support of the Korean American community. After the 1992 Los Angeles Riots, Dr. Hong dedicated his time to promoting harmony and understanding between cultures. He's supported various schools, organizations, and youth-related charities. From 1999 to 2001, Dr. Hong served as chairman of the board of directors at Wilshire Elementary School in Los Angeles, the only predominantly Korean American public elementary school in Southern California at the time.[150]

Dr. Hong also served as the chairman of the Dosan Ahn Chang Ho Memorial Foundation of America in Riverside, California. Dr. Hong spearheaded a statue memorial project of Dosan through its many stages of fundraising, construction, installation, and dedication in Riverside's City Mall on August 11, 2001.

In 2002, Dr. Hong established the Bright World Foundation, a non-profit organization dedicated to creating optimism for the future and to inspire the human spirit. Today, Dr. Hong continues his work through his nonprofit the M&L Hong Foundation.

---

[150] Recorded interview with Dr. Myung Ki "Mike" Hong at his DuraCoat business offices in Riverside on November 9, 2016. Interviewed by Edward T. Chang and Carol K. Park.

CHAPTER 7

MODERN KOREAN AMERICANS AND THE ROAD AHEAD

After the L.A. Riots, Korean American political activity increased dramatically. As a result, Korean Americans now sit on city councils, serve as mayors, and hold important positions in the United States government. During the 1990s, Korean Americans mobilized their political efforts, dramatically increasing their participation on the local and national levels.[151] As Korean Americans rebuilt their lives in the aftermath of the 1992 L.A. Riots, moved to areas including the Inland region of Southern California and San Francisco in Northern California, they continued to be socially and politically vocal. For example, the National Association of Korean Americans was founded in 1994 and is a non-profit, civil and human rights organization of concerned Korean Americans; Chicago-based Korean American Resource and Cultural Center (KRCC) was founded 1995 (KRCC merged with Korean American Community Services in 2017 to form the HANA Center). Through civic and political activism, Korean Americans found themselves threaded into the fabric of American society.

Efforts to promote Korean American identity and visibility included the installation of a statue of Dosan Ahn Chang Ho in downtown Riverside, California, in 2001. Elected in 2015, David Ryu was the first Korean

---

[151] Lee, EunSook. "The Political Awakening of Korean Americans." In *Koreans in the Windy City*, ed. Hyock Chun, Kwang Chung Kim, and Shin Kim, 338-339. East Rock Institute for the Centennial Publication Committee of Chicago, New Haven, Conn. 2005.

American member of the Los Angeles City Council. Jane Jungyon Kim was the first Korean American elected official in San Francisco where she represents District 6 on the Board of Supervisors. Mark Lee Keam has been a member of the Virginia House of Delegates since 2010. Sukhee Kang served as the mayor of Irvine, California, from 2008 to 2012. Michelle Rhee served as chancellor of the Washington D.C. public schools from 2007 to 2010. In 2005, Sam Yoon became the first Asian American and Korean American to be elected to the Boston City Council. The Council of Korean Americans formed in 2015 and is comprised of prominent business owners, politicians, academics, and others who work to raise the voice of Korean Americans in the American public sphere.

Members of the Council of Korean Americans met in Chicago in 2015 and spoke with United States Senator Ladda Tammy Duckworth (D-IL).

According to 2018 population data, the Korean American community is about 1.8 million strong. Koreatown in Los Angeles is now a cultural enclave that attracts people from multiple ethnic backgrounds. The *Hallyu* Wave—an interest in Korean drama, music, and culture—gained momentum in the United States during the 2000s. Korean pop singer Psy helped propel the *Hallyu* Wave into the American spotlight with his song "Gangam Style" in 2013. Los Angeles was home to the KCON USA convention in 2018; the event showcases all things Korean. The convention attracted 85,000 people.[152] Today, Korean barbeque, the bulgogi taco, and Korean drama and music are now part of mainstream American culture.

Korean American actors are also more visible. Sandra Oh, Steven Yeun, Grace Park, Justin Chon, John Cho, and others, are now included in major Hollywood television shows and films. Korean American cuisine, music, and dramas also hit mainstream American culture hard. Los Angeles' Koreatown is an ethnic enclave frequented by a variety of people visiting for the food, shopping, and nightlife. The Korean American community has come a long way since the days of the pioneering Hawaiian sugar plantation workers, the Korean War, and the 1992 Los Angeles Riots, but the road ahead is still paved with obstacles. Korean Americans still face racism and poverty, discrimination, and neglect by politicians who care little for this small community. Korean Americans are still struggling to fight the redistricting of their communities. Also, 22 percent of the Korean American population is without health insurance; 14 percent live below the poverty line; 20 percent of the 65 years and older Koreans live below the poverty line as well, and 38 percent have limited English proficiency, according to a 2016 National Asian American Survey For Korean Americans. Eighty-eight percent of Korean Americans also reported experiencing at least one micro-aggression on a monthly basis, according to the same report.[153]

Yet, while first generation immigrants remain conservative and evangelical Christians, the 1.5- and second-generation Korean Americans are shifting toward change. Korean Americans are dynamic and undergoing social and political transformations as they begin to move toward Democratic voting patterns, liberal ideologies, and a higher sense of community. The future of the Korean American community lies within the children of the first generation of immigrants and the second- and third-generation Korean Americans who can bridge the cultural and

---

[152] Dobuzinskis, Alex. "With K-pop back in U.S. spotlight, Korean-American stars take hope." Reuters. August 11, 2018. https://in.reuters.com/article/us-usa-korea-kpop/with-k-pop-back-in-u-s-spotlight-korean-american-stars-take-hope-idINKBN1KW0KD.

[153] Lee, Taeku. "Korean Americans in the Wake of Sa-I Gu: Where are We 25 Years Later?" Keynote Address at the "Sa-I Gu: The Los Angeles Uprisings 25 Years Later" conference. UCLA, Luskin Conference Center, Los Angeles. April 28, 2017.

generational gaps, speak up politically and socially, and raise their voices to better their community and pave the way for future generations.

Korean Americans are a visible part of American society today. From politics to cuisine, to music and art, Korean Americans now have an identity that is recognized throughout the world. Prior to 1992, Koreans in the United States saw themselves as Korean nationals; today they are Korean Americans.

Mrs. Son Park and her grandson Nathan Young Park in 2013. The future of Korean Americans lies within the hands of the youth as the older generation begins to retire and pass away.

Korean American Population by Decade[154]

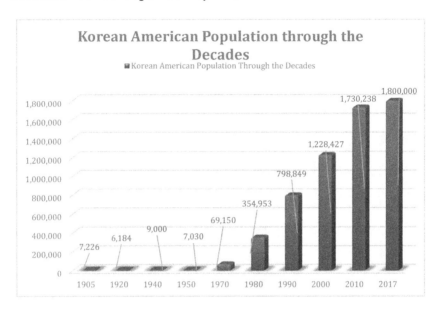

Korean American Population through the Decades

■ Korean American Population Through the Decades

---

[154] Min, Pyong Gap. "Growth of the Korean Population and Changes in their Settlement Patterns of Time, 1990-2008." Queens College and the Graduate Center of CUNY and Chigon Kim, Wright State University:
U.S. Census Bureau, Census 2000 Summary File 2, (SF2). U.S. Census Bureau, 2010 American Community Survey. "Korean-American Population 1910 – 2010." KoreanAmericanStory.org. November 23, 2011. http://koreanamericanstory.org/korean-american-population-1910-2010/.
Korean American population data for 1950 is for Hawaii only and 1960 data was not broken down by the U.S. Census Bureau at the time.

NOTABLE KOREAN AMERICANS BIBLIOGRAPHY

Ahn, Chang Ho – He was a famous and revered leader in the Korean independence movement. He was also a scholar and writer whose work influenced and changed the face of Korean American history. While Ahn lived in the Untied States, he established the first Koreatown USA in Riverside, California sometime in 1904-1905. Ahn was born in 1878 and lived and worked in the United States until he was deported in 1926 after being falsely accused of being a Bolshevist. He lived in China and was later arrested by the Japanese government, illegally extradited to Korea, convicted, and tortured. He was released by the Japanese authorities because they feared he would die. He was then sent to Seoul National University Hospital where he passed away in March 1938. (See Korean American Highlight in Chapter 2).

Ahn, Helen – The wife of Dosan Ahn Chang Ho. Lee Hye-ryon (Helen) was born in Pyongyang, Korea, on April 21, 1884. She and Dosan traveled to the United States in 1902. She and her husband were the first Korean couple to arrive in America. Helen supported the Korean independence movement and worked hard while her husband traveled for the cause. She had five children: Philip, Philson, Susan, Soorah, and Ralph Ahn. She died on April 21, 1969 and is buried with her husband at Dosan Park in South Korea.

Ahn, Philip – The eldest child of Dosan Ahn Chang Ho and Helen Ahn. He became well known for his acting and was the first Korean American to receive a star on the Hollywood Walk of Fame. He died on February 28, 1978.

Ahn, Ralph – The youngest child of Dosan and Helen Ahn. He is a Korean American community leader and an actor.

Ahn, Won Kiu – A successful businessman. Born in 1877, he grew pineapples on land he leased in Ahuimanu, Oahu, Hawaii in the early 1900s. He played an instrumental role in the founding of the Korean National Association and was later awarded the National Foundation Medal by the Republic of South Korea. Ahn died in 1947.

Ahn-Cuddy, Susan – Born on January 16, 1915, she was the eldest daughter of Dosan and Helen Ahn. She was the first female gunnery officer in the United States Navy and served during World War II. She was a Korean American leader and mentor. She died on June 24, 2015.

Buffman, Soorah – Born in 1917 in Los Angeles, she was the second daughter of Dosan and Helen Ahn. She started a popular restaurant called Phil Ahn's Moongate in San Fernando Valley, Panorama City, California.

Charr, Easurk Emsen – Born in 1895, he migrated to Hawaii in 1904 and served in the U.S. military. He is best known for his book, *The Golden Mountain: the Autobiography of a Korean Immigrant, 1895-1960*, which was published in 1961. He died in 1986.

Hong, Myung Ki – A successful businessman and Korean American community leader. He moved to the United States in 1954 and earned a degree in chemistry from the University of California, Los Angeles, in 1959. He founded Dura Coat Products Inc. in 1986. Dr. Hong was instrumental in erecting the Dosan Ahn Chang Ho statue in Riverside, California, in 2001.

Jaisohn, Philip – He was a revered and respected Korean independence and Korean American community leader who was the first Korean to obtain American citizenship in 1890. He was also a practicing physician. Jaisohn convened the First Korean Congress in Philadelphia in April 1919. (See Korean American Highlight in Chapter 1).

Jang, In-whan – Born in Pyongyang, Korea, on March 30, 1875, he was a Korean independence activist best known for his role in the assassination of American diplomat Durham White Stevens. Chang murdered Stevens in San Francisco on March 23, 1908. He was found guilty of second-degree murder and sentenced to 25 years in prison. He was released in 1919 after serving only 10 years. In 1930, Chang committed suicide in San Francisco where he is buried. He was posthumously awarded the Order of Merit for National Foundation by the Ministry of Patriots and Veterans Affairs of South Korea in 1962. His remains were exhumed in 1975 and reburied at Seoul National Cemetery.

Kim, Chang-joon Jay – Born on March 27, 1939, in Seoul, Korea, Kim was the first Korean American to serve in the United States Congress. A Republican, he was a member of the United States House of Representatives from California's 41st District from January 1993 to January 1999. He immigrated to the U.S. in 1961 and graduated from the University of Southern California with a degree in engineering. He also earned a doctorate in political science from Hanyang University in Korea. In 1976, he founded JAYKIM Engineers.

Kim, Chong-lim – Born in 1884, Kim was the first Korean American millionaire known as the "Rice King." He was a Korean independence activist who played an instrumental role in the funding and founding of the Willows Korean Aviation School and Corps in Northern California. He also co-founded the Young Korean Academy with Dosan Ahn Chang Ho in 1913. He died in 1973.

Kim, Elaine – Born on February 26, 1945, in New York, Kim is an award-winning writer, editor, and professor of Asian American Studies at the University of California, Berkeley. She is the co-founder of Asian Women United of California and of the Oakland Korean Community Center. She received a lifetime achievement award from the Association for Asian American Studies in 2011. She was also inducted into the Hall of Outstanding Women in California in 1995.

Kim, Harry – Born in 1939, he is the son of In Kee Kim, one of the first Korean sugar plantation workers in Hawaii. Harry Kim was appointed Civil Defense chief for Hawaii in 1976, a position he held for 24 years. Later, Kim became the mayor of Hawaii County in 2001 as a Republican. He held the post until 2008. He ran for office again in 2016 as an independent and won.

Lee, George (Eng-ho) – Born in Chemulpo (Icheon), Korea, in 1896, Lee was the first Korean pilot. Lee and his father migrated to the United States in 1903. When World War I broke out in 1914, Lee wanted to enlist. When he was 18, he joined the U.S. Army and became a pilot. By 1918, he had flown 156 missions. After the war ended, Lee lived in New York, got married, and had a son.

Lim, John – Born on December 23, 1935, in Yeoju, Gyeonoggi-do, Korea, Lim is a Republican politician who served in both houses of the Oregon Legislative Assembly. He was also the majority leader of the Oregon Senate in 1995. Lim emigrated to the United States in 1966 and received a Master of Divinity from Western Evangelical Seminary in 1970.

Lee, Kyung Won – Born in 1928, "K.W." Lee was a pioneering reporter who is considered the godfather of Asian American journalism. Lee is best known for his work on the Chol Soo Lee case during the 1970s and his publication of the *Koreatown Weekly* and the *Korea Times* English Edition newspapers. (See Korean American Highlight in Chapter 5).

Lee, Sammy – Dr. Samuel "Sammy" Lee was the first Asian American man to win gold during the 1948 Olympic Games in London. He won gold again during the 1952 Olympic Games in Helsinki. Dr. Lee was born on August 1, 1920 in Fresno, California. He had four siblings and was the youngest of the children. Dr. Lee served in the U.S. military and was an ear, nose, throat physician. He married Rosalind M.K. Young; together they had two children, one boy and one girl. Dr. Lee was good friends with Col. Young Oak Kim. Dr. Lee retired in 1990 from his practice in Orange County after 35 years. He died in December 2016.

Lee, Yong-keun – Born in Gang-su Gun, Pyong-an Nam-do in 1890, Lee arrived in the United States in 1916 and moved to Los Angeles in 1917. He was a member of the Young Korean Academy. He was one of the first two aviation officers appointed by the Korean Provisional Government in Shanghai on July 18, 1921. He graduated from Redwood City Aviation School in June 1920 and later attended the Willows Korean Aviation School and Corps. After the Willows school was shuttered in 1921, he went to Sacramento Aviation School to continue his studies. Lee returned to Korea in 1923, where he died in 1950.

Oh, Angela E. – Born in 1955, Oh is a Korean American attorney, teacher, writer, and activist. She is best known for her role as a spokesperson for the Korean American community after the 1992 Los Angeles Riots. In 1997, President Bill Clinton appointed her to One America in the 21st Century: The President's Initiative on Race.

Oh, Bonnie Bongwon – Born in South Korea, Oh emigrated to the United States for her education and earned a Ph.D. in East Asian history from the University of Chicago. She is currently a distinguished professor of Korean studies at Georgetown University. Her 38 years of teaching at the university level are peppered with milestones including her work on comfort women, women and girls forced into sexual slavery by the Imperial Japanese Army before and during World War II.

Ohr, Fred – Born on July 15, 1919, in Idaho, Ohr was a highly decorated flying ace during World War II. He joined the U.S. military in 1938. He was deployed in 1942 with the 68th Material Service Squadron U.S. Army Air Corp. He flew missions with the 2nd Fighter Squadron, 52nd Fighter Group, and was its squadron commanding officer. After the war, he became a dental surgeon and lived in Chicago. He died on September 6, 2015.

Park, Hee-sung – Born on May 8, 1896 in Haeju, Hwanghae Province, Korea, Park was one of the two first aviation officers appointed by the Korean Provisional Government in Shanghai. He emigrated to the United States in 1918 and went by the American name Howard. He began training as a pilot at the Willows Korean Aviation School and Corps in Northern California when it opened in early 1920. When the Willows School closed in 1921, he went to an aviation school in Sacramento, where he trained with Lee Young-keun. Today, the Korean Air Force recognizes the Willows Korean Aviation School and Corps as its origins. Park was an exceptional pilot according to newspaper reports. However, due to a mechanical malfunction, his plane crashed during his examination and he barely survived. Three weeks after his accident, he retook the exam and passed on May 22, 1921. Lee lived a quiet life and suffered from injuries he sustained from the accident. He died in 1937.

Park, Yong-man – Born on July 2, 1881, in Cheorwon, Gangwon, Korea, Park emigrated to the United States in 1904. He was a Korean independence activist who established various Korean nationalist organizations in the U.S., including a Korean military academy in Hastings, Nebraska. He also founded the Korean Military Corps. in Hawaii. He also joined the American Expeditionary Force and was sent to Siberia in 1918. When he completed his military service, he went to Shanghai, China, in 1920. He was assassinated on October 17, 1928, by a Korean communist.

Rhee, Syngman – Born in March 1875, Rhee was the first president of South Korea and a well-known Korean American leader. Rhee was the first Korean American to earn a doctorate's degree when he graduated from Princeton University in 1910. He spent significant time in the United States lobbying for Korea's independence during the early 1900s. However, Rhee's political career was riddled with controversy. He was forced to resign his presidency in 1960 and fled South Korea to Hawaii, where he lived in exile until his death in 1965. (See Korean American Highlight in Chapter 1).

Song, Alfred H. – Born on February 16, 1919, in Hawaii, Song was the first Korean American and Asian American to serve on the California state legislature. He won election to the state assembly in 1961 and in 1966 moved to the state senate. A lawyer by trade, he was revered for his expertise. By 1978, his career had come to an end, after an FBI investigation that was later dropped. Song died in October 2004.

KOREAN AMERICAN HISTORY: SHORT TIMELINE OF EVENTS

May 22, 1882 - U.S.-Korea signed the Treaty of Amity, Commerce, and Navigation.

January 13, 1903 - Arrival of 102 Korean immigrants in Honolulu, Hawaii.

1903 - The Friendship Society is established in San Francisco, California.

March 23, 1904 - Ahn Chang Ho moved to Riverside, California.

1905 - The Gongnip Hyophoe (Cooperative Association) is established.

1909 - Park Yong-man establishes the Korean Youth Military Academy in Hastings, Nebraska.

1904-1918 - Pachappa Camp: The First Koreatown in the United States is founded by Dosan Ahn Chang Ho and flourishes until the 1913 citrus freeze. However, the Koreatown persists until it finally dwindles out of existence in 1918.

March 23, 1908 - Jang In-hwan assassinates Durham White Stevens.

February 1, 1909 - The Korean National Association is established.

June 25, 1913 - The Hemet Valley Incident involving 11 Koreans occurs in Hemet, California. The Korean laborers faced racism and were run out of town by a group of white workers who thought they were Japanese. The incident would capture headlines and change the status of Koreans in the United States.

July 2, 1913 - Secretary of State William Jennings Bryan announced that "Koreans are not Japanese subjects" after David Lee, the Korean National Association president, sent a telegram to the secretary declaring the matter had been resolved by the Korean community. Lee also declared that Koreans in America were not Japanese.

1919 - Several Korean women organizations are established.

April 1919 - The Korean Provisional Government is established in Shanghai, China.

March 1, 1919 - Peaceful protests erupt throughout Korea against Japanese colonization.

January 1920 - Hwang Hye-su organizes the Korean Mothers Club at the Korean department at the International Institute of the YWCA. She helps immigrant women learn English and the logistics of running a household in America. The Korean YWCA exists until 1943.

March 1920 - The Willows Korean Aviation School/Corps is founded in Willows, California.

May 10, 1921 - The Korean Student Association forms in Honolulu, Hawaii.

June 2, 1921 - The KNA of North America publishes a three volume Korean textbook in San Francisco.

May 15, 1924 - The U.S. Congress passes the Johnson-Reed Immigration Act, which prohibits immigration from Asian countries, excluding Japan and the Philippines. The act becomes known as the Oriental Exclusion Act and prohibits the naturalization of Asians and bars the entrance of Korean picture brides to the United States. Korean students in America are forced to return to their home country after completing their studies.

June 29, 1928 - Chang Deok-su, Yoon Chi-yeong, Hong Deuk-su, Lee Bong-su, Huh Jeong, and Kim Yang-su publish *Korean Nationalist Weekly (Samil Sinbo)* in New York. Kim Yang-su serves as editor in chief.

October 15, 1931 - To preserve and support Korean culture, Korean students and residents of New York establish the Korean Cultural Association at Earl Hall of Columbia University. They open a library, boasting nearly 1,000 works.

1936 - Philip Ahn stars in his first film *Anything Goes*. Also, Fred Anderson grants the Kim Brothers the exclusive right to grow and sell his patented nectarine the *Kism*.

September 16, 1940 - President Franklin Roosevelt signs the Selective Service and Training Act into law, the first peace time draft in American history. Despite their ineligibility to volunteer for service, Korean American men are subject to the draft.

1944 - Young Oak Kim leads the 100th/442nd infantry battalion comprised of primarily Japanese American soldiers in Italy and France.

1947 - A new law allows spouses of American citizens to enter the United States, opening immigration for war brides.

August 5, 1948 - Sammy Lee won the gold medal in the men's 10-meter platform diving event at the London Olympics. This makes him the first Asian American man to win gold for the United States.

June 25, 1950 - The Korean War breaks out and Col. Young Oak Kim reenlists in the U.S. Army.

September 22, 1955 - Chong Sung-gu and his family immigrate to the United States as the first Korean war refugees.

October 1955 - Harry Holt brings eight adopted children to the United States from Korea.

April 12, 1960 - Alfred Song is elected to the city council of Monterrey Park. He is the first person of Korean ancestry to obtain such a position.

1962 - The Republic of Korea honors posthumously Ahn Chang-ho with the founder's medal, which his wife Helen Ahn accepts on his behalf at a ceremony in Los Angeles. Their eldest son, Philip Ahn becomes honorary mayor of Panorama City. Rhee Joon opens the first Taekwondo studio in Washington, D.C.

October 3, 1965 - The Hart-Celler Act of 1965 is passed, eliminating the old national quota system and permitting larger numbers of Asian immigrants to enter the United States.

March 13, 1970 - Radio Korea broadcasts from 9 a.m. to 10 p.m. daily.

April 16, 1970 - Martha Holt, wife of the late Harry Holt, brings the five thousandth Korean orphan to the United States to be adopted into an American family.

December 17, 1971 - President Richard Nixon appoints Herbert Y. C. Choy to the United States Court of Appeals for the Ninth Circuit, making Choy the first Asian American named to a federal court.

March 29, 1972 - Los Angeles Koreatown launches a Korean sign campaign. Fifty-one stores hang Korean language signs in compliance.

April 1977 - Groundbreaking occurs for Architect David Hyun's (first generation) design of Los Angeles's Little Tokyo plaza.

November 24, 1977 - Kim Myeong-gyun, the first female Korean American attorney, opens an office in Chicago.

1979 - African Americans lead boycotts of Korean owned businesses in Manhattan, Harlem, and Queens. Tensions between the two communities rise and the so-called "black-Korean" conflict grows.

May 26, 1980 - Korean American students stage a blood donation drive at the Los Angeles Red Cross. Approximately 200 Korean American students and supporters participate, demanding their blood be sent to the city of Gwangju, where protests for democracy erupted. The Korean Red Cross refuses to accept the blood. Without permission from the Korean Red Cross, the donations cannot be sent to Korea. Local TV networks cover the story.

August 10, 1983 - Chol Soo Lee, who was wrongfully convicted of murder in San Francisco, is released. The case drew national attention and created a Pan-Asian movement.

1987 - Korean immigration to the United States reaches a historic high, when 32,135 Koreans legally enter the United States.

April 29, 1992 - The Los Angeles riots erupted after the release of the Rodney King verdict. During four days of rioting, 2,000-2,500 Korean businesses in Los Angeles sustained damage or were destroyed, totaling about $400 million in damages. One Korean American, Edward Lee died from a gunshot wound.

November 4, 1992 - Jay Kim is elected to the U.S. House of Representatives from California's 41st District. He is the first Korean American to serve in the House of Representatives. Yong-geun "John" Lim is elected to the Oregon Senate, Jackie Young is reelected to the Hawaii state legislature, and Paul Shin is elected to the Washington State House of Representatives.

March 1, 1993 - The Washington Coalition for Comfort Women Issues, Inc., sponsors a street demonstration in front of the Japanese Embassy for "Peace and Right" to commemorate the March First Movement. Comfort women included many Korean and Chinese girls and women who were forced into sexual slavery for Japanese soldiers before and during the Second World War. In Japanese, they were euphemistically referred to as "comfort women" because they were intended to comfort the soldiers.

March 31, 1993 - Ronald T.Y. Moon becomes Chief Justice of the Supreme Court of Hawaii, making him the first Korean to hold the position in America.

September 14, 1994 - Margaret Cho's sitcom *All-American Girl* premiers on ABC. The show focuses on her life at the center of a Korean American family.

May 1995 - SAT II Korean is formalized

1997 - Koreans have the highest self-employment rate in the United States

June 1997 - President Bill Clinton appoints Angela Oh to the President's Initiative on Race. She serves on a seven-member advisory board to the president charged with examining how race, racism, and racial differences have affected the United States.

1998 - Lela Lee's *Angry Little Asian Girl* comic airs as a short film.

June 5, 1999 - The "Go for Broke" Monument is unveiled in Los Angeles, featuring the name of every Japanese American who fought in World War II. Colonel Young Oak Kim serves on the planning commission of the monument, which honors the men of his battalion.

November 7, 2000 - Republican Harry Kim is elected mayor of Hawaii County. He ran as a Republican but identified as an independent. He was mayor from 2001-2008. He ran again in 2016 as an independent and won.

February 13, 2001 - Phil Yu launches his *Angry Asian Man* blog to combat racism and fight the stereotypes he and several friends encountered at Northwestern University.

August 11, 2001 - City officials inaugurate a memorial statue of Ahn Chang Ho in Riverside, California.

2003 - President George W. Bush issues a proclamation celebrating the 100th anniversary of Korean immigration to the United States. In 2005, the House and Senate passed resolutions supporting Korean American Day which is celebrated on January 13.

May 2003 - Chun Jong Joon wins a four-year legal battle against discriminatory visa regulations against Koreans. Owing to fears that individuals who had applied for permanent visas would stay in the country, the U.S. systematically denied applicants for visitors' visas who had previously applied for permanent visas. Joon's victory succeeded in abolishing the practice.

June 26, 2003 - George Pataki, the governor of New York, announces "the Year of Korean Immigrants" in 2003. At the commemoration, Korean immigrants in New York hold a photo exhibition and a festival for the 100th anniversary of Korean immigration and publish a book, *The 100th Anniversary of Koreans in New York.*

December 29, 2005 - Young Oak Kim dies and is buried at Punchbowl National Cemetery in Honolulu, Hawaii.

May 6, 2008 - A statue of Philip Jaisohn is constructed in Sheridan Circle Park in front of the Korean Embassy in Washington, D.C.

September 2010 - The Young Oak Kim Center for Korean American Studies at the University of California Riverside is established.

June 3, 2014 - Los Angeles County provides voting kiosks with instructions in Korean for the first time in its primary elections.

August 4, 2014 - Union City, New Jersey, erects a memorial for comfort women, though the Japanese government protests the dedication.

2015 - David Ryu is elected to the Los Angeles City Council. He is the first Korean to hold a seat on the council.

2016 - A book on Korean American oral histories is translated into Korean and published in Korea. *Lonesome Journey: The Korean American Century* was written by K.W. Lee and translated by Edward T. Chang.

April 2017 - The 25th anniversary of the 1992 Los Angeles Riots is commemorated. Media covers the Korean American story in depth, for the first time since the riots.

2018 - Korean American Chloe Kim makes history as the youngest woman to win an Olympic snowboarding medal during the Winter Olympic Games in PyeongChang, South Korea in February 2018.

ABOUT THE AUTHORS

Author Edward T. Chang is a Professor of Ethnic Studies at the University of California Riverside and the founding Director of the Young Oak Kim Center for Korean American Studies at UCR. He is an established author with more than 10 published works including *Korean American Pioneer Aviators: The Willows Airmen,* a respected academic, and has been the voice of the Korean American community for more than 25 years.

Author Carol K. Park is a researcher at the YOK Center for Korean American Studies at UCR and is considered an expert in her field. She is also a filmmaker, an award-winning journalist, and holds a Master of Fine Arts in creative writing. Park is also the author of *Memoir of a Cashier: Korean Americans, Racism, and Riots.*

INDEX

www.ingramcontent.com/pod-product-compliance
Lightning Source LLC
LaVergne TN
LVHW040136060125
800587LV00001B/5